Chronicles of a Bering Sea Captain

Chronicles of a Bering Sea Captain

To all my friends, at Sacred Rain! Love you,

Jake

Jake Jacobsen

ISBN-13: 9781523639540
ISBN-10: 1523639547
Library of Congress Control Number: 2016901475
CreateSpace Independent Publishing Platform
North Charleston, South Carolina

To PJ
For always making me promise to come back and always being there when I did.

AUTHOR'S NOTE

As you read this book, you may find it helpful and informative to pull up www.beringseacaptain.com. The "Chapter by Chapter" media section, found by clicking on the "Learn More" button on the home page (or by simply scrolling down), was designed as a companion to this book. The section includes photographs, notes, videos, and links relevant to each chapter.

The website also includes a form for sending comments and questions, and other items you may find interesting. I would like to know what stories resonate with readers as well those things that require a more thorough explanation. Thank you for your interest in this book and in the incredible world of Bering Sea fishing.

TABLE OF CONTENTS

PREFACE

The Bering Sea is a cold corner of the earth that claims the lives of many men and women who risk everything to chase a dream, pursue adventure, and bolster their bank account. Most come to make as much money as they can in the shortest time possible, and get out.

Some of us stay, intoxicated by the money, seduced by the challenge, and provoked by the possibilities available on this rugged frontier. Many of us can't cope with a nine to five job routine. For most, there are few other prospects as promising.

Why did I fish the Bering Sea for so long? It's complicated. Fishing was part of my family and my childhood. Perhaps it was the addictive nature of constant short but satisfying stimuli, despite the collateral costs of family life and comfort. Another factor was the ease of obtaining work in an industry where few possess the required skills, accompanied by persistent pressure to pay bills.

The Bering Sea fishing industry is a fascinating domain that I've tried to document accurately through this series of stories from my experience spanning five decades of involvement. Starting as a child playing in the shipyard and sailing on my father's old wooden trawler since the age of seven, I found my first full-pay fishing job as a fourteen-year-old deckhand on my father's boat. At fifteen, I worked on the largest fishing vessel in the United States, a 300-foot factory trawler. At seventeen, I went to the Bering Sea to try crab fishing. I was the engineer on my father's new crab boat the next year. A few years later, the boat was tied to the Pan Alaska pot loading dock in Dutch Harbor, preparing to go crab fishing far down the Aleutian chain. My father, the captain, walked down the dock to where I was repairing a crab pot. "I've got to go home and take care of some business," he said. "You are the captain now. You know what to do." I may have known what to do, but sometimes knowledge is not enough. I was fortunate to always bring the boat and its crew back to the dock.

A well-educated mechanical engineer who I once took crab fishing remarked, "If I had not seen it for myself I would have never believed that anyone, anywhere, any place in the world, worked this hard." Before the televising of crab fishing, few people were interested in the stories I told. The setting was simply too foreign to their experience to be credible. Now, with television providing pictures of crab pots, pot launchers, icy decks, waves reaching over and crashing on the crew, and perilous fishing through storms and in vast expanses of ice, stories I once told to blank and unbelieving stares are suddenly exciting and relevant. I hope readers find them that way as well. All of these adventures actually happened, and I have taken pains to avoid exaggeration.

This book recounts the sea time of a reluctant sailor starting as a young greenhorn, emerging as a confident captain, and aging as a fishermen's advocate and friend. The stories relate one life's involvement in an interesting industry. Like many adventures on the high seas, they are about unique, funny, or difficult circumstances, determined endurance, and a serially dangerous dance with nature's many moods. These are my stories, but more importantly, they are my perspective of an industry forged from a collection of similar stories. Far more harrowing tales told by better fishermen than I, will never find a voice, and countless acts of courage and strength are captured forever in the depths of the Bering Sea. My stories are a glimpse into the lives of thousands who will never find the words to describe what they did, what they saw, and what they felt.

Not confined to crab fishing, my experience includes captaining vessels in all of the large-boat fisheries of the Bering Sea and some of the west coast fisheries. In all of the Bering Sea fisheries, it includes running both catcher-only boats as well as boats that catch and process their product at sea. Fish tendering, running a tugboat, participating in research charters, and working as a marine surveyor, price negotiator for the crab fleet, and Executive Director of the Bering Sea's largest cooperative of crab fishermen, round out my resume. As a teenager, I didn't plan on spending so much of my life at sea, and I never imagined I would grow up to be a fisherman. But life happened quickly. Suddenly I found myself both grown up, and a fisherman. In retrospect, I am grateful to be associated with, and numbered among, an amazing group of people.

Finally, it takes an abundance of arrogance to challenge the Bering Sea on a crab boat. I was not the greatest fishermen, nor was I the sturdiest sailor, although once believing so instilled in me the audacity necessary to face storms, work for days without sleep, and run unflinching into flaming engine rooms. If any residual arrogance resides in these pages, I apologize. My purpose is not to aggrandize myself, but to accurately portray my experience in an extraordinary industry.

INTRODUCTION

The Reach

The night was beautiful. Its clarity revealed an eternity of stars and folded us into the firmament as if we were gliding through the galaxy. The waters of the Strait of Juan de Fuca were uncharacteristically calm. To the east, north, and south, multicolored lights blinked along the shore. To the west, stars arched to the horizon, disappeared into the black carpet of sea, and re-surfaced as long shiny reflections on the rippled water. Shimmering above the mountains of Vancouver Island was a most fantastic display of pulsating rushing aurora. Borealis was out tonight, spreading its magic length across the northern sky. It appeared as a confused colored waterfall, rushing upward. Then it was a giant green glowing curtain, moving as if children played in its folds. Later, it looked like great green searchlights advertising a sale in the starry expanse.

Leaving was always the hardest part of fishing. Even before I was married and long before I had children, it was painful. But now, leaving my family and waving a long, sad goodbye tore at my heart inflicting a wound that would not heal until I was home. But would I return? So many during those years did not.

Would I make the money needed to pay the bills? A mechanical failure, illness, injury, or just poor fishing, could prove financially devastating. But if sorrow clad my departure, determination cast my return in iron resolve. I would come home. I promised my beautiful wife I would.

I remained awake that entire night, guiding the boat through the traffic of ships and sailboats, submarines and scows, each bound for somewhere with a plan and a purpose. I was bound for the Bering Sea to fish king crab in a fishery that would later become known as the most dangerous fishery in the world, and popularized by a reality television show. But for now, a television series about fishing was unimaginable, and the danger lay ahead in the distance. Tonight was a rare moment of stunning beauty, gladdening the soul, and removing some of the sting of separation.

The crew was asleep. They worked the entire night previous preparing for departure. I stood alone in the wheelhouse, alive with the stars, the aurora, and a thousand thoughts. The starboard side window was open. I was counting on the crisp night air to maintain my wakefulness, and along with the sights, I enjoyed the sounds of a calm night.

Dall's porpoises breached as they played before our bow. When I was younger, I loved to watch them dart and weave in front of the boat. Tonight I only listened as the music of their spouting played against the background of the waters parting before us. The porpoise are perfect fishermen. Always fishing, they never need to shut down. Half their brain sleeps while the other half works. The steep seas that torment us are a playground for them. I am jealous.

Listening to the porpoise takes my thoughts back to childhood. As a boy, the crow's nest was my favorite place on the boat. From this protected platform atop a high mast, I spent hours watching the high-speed weaving, darting, and breaching of our porpoise vanguard. I could look out over the vast undulating sea with vision unobstructed. I watched the bow plow through armadas of floating sail-backed jellyfish and searched rafts of seaweed for sleeping seals and otters. I could reach out and touch the wings of gliding gulls and soaring albatross. On calm nights, I watched the enchanting glow of a green carpet of bioluminescent algae, ignited by our intrusion.

The rewards of the crow's nest were well worth the climb. A ladder ran from the starboard bulwark to the mast just below the crow's nest. The ladder was constructed of wooden rungs clamped to steel cables that became progressively smaller toward the top and fastened to the mast below the crow's nest. While the bottom rung of the ladder was four feet wide, the top rung was only eight inches, and right next to the mast. When I reached the top of the cable ladder I had to reach behind my head to grab a three-rung steel ladder that descended from an opening in the silver crow's nest above. I didn't mind the climb on the wobbly cable ladder, although there wasn't much to hold on to at the top where the pitch and roll of the boat are amplified. But I was too small to reach the bottom rung of the crow's nest ladder without first letting go of the cable ladder and reaching up with both hands.

I knew the steel ladder above was solid. It didn't bounce and move like the cable ladder to which I clung so tenaciously. I knew that once I was in the crow's nest, I would be protected. No longer would it be necessary to hold tightly to a small and uncertain stand. For anxious minutes, I would measure the distance, and fear letting go. And then I would gauge the timing and make the reach. Clutching the crow's nest ladder, I could climb into the peaceful perch above. Most of my time fishing felt like climbing to the crows nest—wobbly and uncertain—and that tenuous moment of letting go to try desperately for something better. Nothing was ever secure. Now, having reached the crow's nest of my fishing experience, I look back with a full spectrum of feelings, and peer forward at what seems to be a favorable future for Bering Sea sailors.

Sustainable Seafood

From the dawn of man's desire for prosperity, the sea has whispered seductively of the treasures below its surface. Fishing is the art of using tools to extend our reach into those dark depths, pull out its treasures, and transport them to shore. Until recently, the ocean's supply of seafood seemed inexhaustible. Now we realize that the ocean's bounty can continue only to the extent that sustainability science effectively manages stocks, and governments make and enforce responsible regulations.

The tiny trawler that carried me into fishing as a seven-year-old took a diminutive and quickly replenished dip into the vast stocks of West Coast groundfish. But I recall counting lines of foreign super-trawlers fishing off our coast. Eight, ten, sometimes fourteen in a row, their massive nets swept the seabed without restraint. The Magnuson-Stevens Fisheries Conservation and Management Act of 1976 was the dawn of a new day for sustainable fishing in the United States, but even before that, the State of Alaska practiced principles of sustainable seafood harvesting within its jurisdiction. The Alaska State Constitution mandates sustainability. For the fisheries described herein, the temptation to take treasure from the sea was and continues to be tempered by reason and regulation. Stock stability is not only a matter of stewardship but also a commercial concern for fishermen with long-term capital investments.

Following my father and my grandfathers, I sailed the seas to find fortune but I also understood the need to frame a future of productive fishing. Stories herein of working to the limits of human endurance, of injuries, of lives lost, and of courage found, must be understood in the context of a tightly regulated quota system. The determined and sometimes deadly competition was not for the decimation of the resource, but for harvesting a small fraction of the biomass, as made available by the government after consideration of the best science available. Although frequently blamed for stock declines, Alaskan fishermen harvest only to the extent they are permitted. The allowable harvest of Bering Sea king crab, for example, is typically less than ten percent of the adult male population. Other factors like water temperature, predation, competition, and ocean currents are more likely culprits of stock fluctuation and season closures.

Today there are still places in the world where despicable people ravage the oceans resources, usually in violation of established law. Organized crime, slave traders, and pirates continue to pillage inadequately protected stocks. The remarkably resilient crab resources of the Russian Far East, for example, continue to be targeted by poachers who consistently catch twice the legal quota. But that does not happen in Alaska. Consumers can confidently purchase and enjoy Alaskan seafood, knowing it represents the gold standard of sustainability and quality.

Recent regulatory innovations in the crab fisheries of the Bering Sea created space for crew safety, environmental improvements, and community protections. No longer is crab fishing in the Bering Sea the most dangerous legal occupation in the world. It is now one of the safest and most responsible fisheries in the country. I am grateful to have played a part in those changes. I still worry about my son who fishes crab today, but his chances of coming home alive have greatly improved since my mother saw me sail away from Seattle as a seventeen-year-old bound for the Bering Sea. The stories that follow are from the old "deadliest" days—when days and nights of difficult work tested the limits of mental and physical stamina of the crews. The reality of fisheries management today is much more rational, with catch shares and cooperatives eliminating the all-out, catch at any cost, derby days of the past.

The Bering Sea has challenges ahead. Oil and gas exploration, mining projects, and northward expansion of shipping lanes may change the way its spatial resources are utilized and natural resources are prioritized. They offer new threats to the fragile ecosystem upon which fishermen depend; and fishermen will always be at the forefront of the fight for purity of product, sustainability of stocks and protection of man's ability to extract tasty treasure from the sea.

CHAPTER 1

THE PARAGON

A Seasick Young Sailor

My father was in the Antarctic when the Nazis occupied Norway. He came to the United States and became a naval officer, serving in the Pacific. After the war, he brought his new bride, a bright young nurse from Oklahoma, to Seattle and fished from Oregon to Alaska. He built a fleet of small ships, a fish processing plant on the Seattle waterfront, and a trucking line. But circumstances caused a contraction in the business and by the time I was ready to go to sea, he was down to one boat, the Paragon, a halibut schooner converted to a trawler.

I first tagged along on a fishing trip when I was seven. During the summer months, my brother Charlie and I took turns going out on the boat. We both got seasick. Cramped and queasy, I curled in my bunk for days, emerging only to empty my ever-present bucket, use the head (a nautical term for toilet), or to ask when we would be returning to shore. Often I preferred to lie on the hard, wood deck beneath the galley table, holding to the table post, bucket close at hand. It was warm there.

I endured endless hours of nausea and uncontrollable vomiting with nothing left to expel but green bile and blood. I longed only for stable land. But I kept going back. Why? What makes a young person persist in such unpleasantness? Was it a sense of pride perhaps? My father was a fisherman, as was his father. My mother's father was a fisherman. My uncle was a fisherman. Whatever the reason, my brother and I suffered through our persistent motion sickness and sailed again and again.

Jake Jacobsen

On Charter in Alaska

During the summer of 1969 (when I was fourteen) my father's boat was chartered by the Alaska Department of Fish and Game to collect information on salmon stocks in Southeast Alaska. My father was the captain. Jamie, a twenty-one-year-old family friend, and I were the deckhands. Biologists and a cook completed the crew.

We left Seattle bound for Sitka Alaska, a three-day trip. But the seas were rough and my familiar but abhorrent companion, seasickness, soon afflicted me. My stateroom was below deck in a tiny space converted into a cramped cabin from a corner of the engine room. A half-inch thick sheet of plywood separated my compact cabin from a loud Lister generator engine. The thin wood did little to diminish the constant clatter of the engines, or restrain the offensive odors of the engine room. The creaking planks of the fifty-year-old wooden hull completed the cacophony of noise that cradled me in sleep each night.

On the second day of sullen seasickness, as I lay nauseous in the darkness of my diesel-scented stateroom, I came to a decision. I was paid to do a job and I could not do it disabled by seasickness. But quitting was not in my nature. The only acceptable alternative was putting an end to the seasickness. With all the determination a fourteen-year-old could muster, I left the confines of my miserable cabin, took a shower, and forced down a sandwich. Then I went outside, and made some noise on my banjo. I stayed outside, feasting on fresh air, with eyes on the wall instead of the water, and convinced myself that seasickness was a thing of the past. A second sandwich went down easier. Neither of the sandwiches resurfaced (thank God for peanut butter). I have not been seasick since.

It was a summer of fun and adventure. The typical day started in the wee hours of the morning with pulling in my fishing line (hopefully with a fish on it), hauling up the anchor, and running to a prescribed survey station where the fishing gear was set. After the anchor was up, I went back to bed. We used Japanese floating longline gear. It is illegal to use such gear in Alaska unless you are pursuing a scientific study for the State. It consisted of a red twine interspersed every few feet with a hook dangling from a foot-long leader. We used two types of bait: fresh frozen anchovies and salted dried anchovies, apparently to determine which the fish preferred. After leaving the gear in the water for an hour or two, it was hauled back. Each captured fish was measured, weighed, fit with a tag, and released. I would be called around 8:00 or 9:00 a.m. to drive the boat to the next anchorage. After anchoring, we baited the gear and got it ready for the morning set. For the rest of the afternoon we were free to hike, fish, swim or just hang out and enjoy the surrounding scenery.

Despite the cold water, I occasionally jumped over the side for a swim. When a gentle swell was rolling into the bay, I swung from the boom wire, gaining momentum until I was high over the water where I let go. After one such swing, I was climbing back aboard when a giant whale breached next to the boat, right were I swam just seconds before. I didn't go back in.

My favorite anchorage, and the place we anchored most often, was a little pocket near the end of Puffin Bay. Accessed through a narrow opening, the tiny inlet seemed like a magical place. At the end of the bay, two streams ran through a marshy meadow. Friendly, evergreen-covered mountains shielded the gray water from wind and instilled a feeling of security and seclusion. If I decided to live like a hermit, I thought, I would build a cabin here, in the meadow, between the streams. There was a lake a short hike away. We often took the skiff to the beach and hiked to the lake where we skipped rocks and skinny-dipped in the ice-cold water. On every trip to the beach, I carried a Winchester, model 30-30 lever-action rifle.

Some days I set course for Litulya Bay. A large bay surrounding a bird-covered island, Litulya Bay was the location of a devastating mega-tsunami created when ninety million tons of rock and ice slid into the bay, creating a wave nearly one-hundred feet in height. Hiking through the woods near Litulya Bay, I found a pleasant patch of wild strawberries in a small clearing. I was on the ground, gorging on small but tasty berries when a large wolf entered the clearing, not six feet from me. The wolf froze. I froze. We stared at each other. Where was my rifle? It was just out of reach. I set it down and was too interested in eating the delicious berries to pull it along as I moved in search of more. Would lunging for it provoke an attack? Could I load the chamber in time? Those questions remained unanswered. After several seconds of motionless consideration, the wolf trotted off into the forest, and I did not see it again.

Jamie, Dick (a biologist), and me took the skiff to the beach on another day. Before leaving, none of us checked the level in the gas tank, and as we approached the beach, our old Johnson 10-horsepower outboard motor sputtered, coughed, and died. We paddled the remaining distance to a sandy spot on the beach and pulled the crippled skiff safely beyond the rising tide. Hiking through the woods, we encountered two prospectors panning for gold in a creek. They were teachers by profession but spent their summers searching for precious metals in the Alaskan wilderness. They had not yet struck the mother lode but said they usually made enough to cover the expense of their trip. They loved the rustic lifestyle and the escape from the routine of work and congestion of civilization. We hiked several miles to their camp, where they gave us a heavy can of aviation fuel that worked very well in getting us back to the boat.

Most evenings, wherever we anchored, I set a large hook on a line weighted with an old shackle over the side in hopes of catching a halibut. Many mornings, I was met with the shackle and an empty hook, but sometimes a fish was attached. The strong halibut struggled as they approached the surface, and fought my efforts to pull them aboard by flapping furiously. I needed help pulling the larger fish over the rail.

One morning I effortlessly retrieved the line, certain the shiny silver hook was empty. But soon a great, gray shape surfaced next to the boat. Watching from the wheelhouse, my father grabbed his shotgun and ran to the deck. An old halibut fisherman, he knew a fish this size was far beyond my capacity to handle. A well-placed blast to the head paralyzed the monstrous fish, and my father was able to hoist it aboard with the boom. The fish was much larger than I was. It was donated to the delighted inhabitants of Elfin Cove, Alaska who probably fed it to their dogs. Older halibut are not nearly as fine tasting as younger fish.

Trawling

After the charter, we pulled our odorous nets from the hold and trawled for bottom fish. Trawling involves towing a net at the end of two cables. The

cables wind onto winches on each side of the deck. Attached to the net end
of the cables are steel structures called doors (because they open the net).
There are a variety of door designs, but they all work in the same way. As the
door is pulled through the water, its shape creates drag that forces it outward,
stretching the opening of the net. It also provides weight that helps the net
tend bottom (or remain at the desired depth, depending on the type of door).
Fish funnel into the net and are collected in a specialized double-mesh bag at
the end called the cod end. It's always called a cod end regardless of the kind
of fish it may contain.

Modern trawlers have automatic computer-controlled winches, sensors
that measure the distance between the doors, sonars that reveal the fish in
front of the net, and sensors that report when the cod end is full. We had none
of those technologies. Hauling the net back to the boat, we laid the wire level
on the winch by muscle-operated pipes, forcing it to one side or the other.
Properly winding the wire on the winch was critical to avoiding backlashes
when setting it out again. Although I tried my best to control the stubborn
cable, both setting and hauling back seemed like things that just happened
instead of things I did.

The Paragon did not have a stern ramp (a ramp cut into the stern allowing the cod end to be pulled on board the boat). The Paragon was backward.
Built as a halibut schooner, it had the house at the stern. Boats built as trawlers
typically have the house forward, leaving a large working area aft for retriev-
ing and working on nets, and a ramp at the stern for bringing the catch on
board. An aft house provides a more comfortable ride, and the captain can
watch the deck from the wheelhouse. A stern ramp was not practical on the
Paragon. The galley was in the way. This shortcoming required the captain to
maneuver the boat alongside the net while the crew prayed that the cod end
would not sink before they could bring it the fish aboard. The boom wire was
hooked into a strap, and the fish were winched aboard. With the pull of a line,
the captured fish flowed onto the deck. A good tow required five, six or more
splits (lifts) to bring all the fish aboard.

After emptying the cod end, the only way to get around the deck was
to wade through thousands of scaly fish, each one equipped with numerous

sharp spines. But I worried more about wolf eels. Wolf eels slithered straight to the bottom of the pile. I was certain their vise-like jaws were eager for a taste of my tender toes. The wolf eels and other unmarketable fish were discarded while "money fish" was sorted by species into bins in the fish hold below the deck and covered with ice. If the net was slightly damaged, as it frequently was, it was rolled off the net reel at the stern and mended there. If it was shredded into strings, it was pulled forward of the house where, once the fish were put away, there was more room for repair. The hours on deck seemed endless. After finishing one deck-load of fish, it was time to haul the net back and do it all again. After four or five days with just a few hours sleep, I was exhausted but happy. This was my first full-share job as a crewman on a boat and I was determined to do as well as the adults. But things got worse. Jamie threw a large red snapper at me as a prank. Instinctively, I raised my right hand to deflect the fish. A four-inch-long dorsal spine pierced my little finger, ran down the bone and exited near the knuckle. The pain was excruciating. Within the hour, my hand was purple, swollen, and unusable. Now, my appreciation for good fishing, fine weather, and fascinating fish species was gone. I focused only on my aching arm, throbbing hand, and desire to be done. Suddenly, I hated trawling.

CHAPTER 2

THE SEAFREEZE PACIFIC

Fighting in the Factory

They were vessels ahead of their time. Built in Maryland by Isbrandsten Steamship Lines (American Stern Trawlers) in 1969 (becoming operational in 1970), the Seafreeze Atlantic and the Seafreeze Pacific were the first American factory trawlers and at 295-feet in length, the largest fishing vessels in the country. Harry Jacobsen (my uncle) was captain of the Seafreeze Atlantic and fished out of Boston. Erling Jacobsen (my father) was captain of the Seafreeze Pacific, fishing on the West Coast.

A factory trawler (sometimes called a catcher-processor) is a vessel that catches fish and renders them into something a consumer is more likely to put on her plate, like a fillet. Some produce surimi, a fish paste used in products intended to taste like crab or lobster meat. Others simply remove the heads and entrails and freeze the fish for further processing. Both of the Seafreeze ships were designed to catch fish and produce individual quick frozen fish fillets at sea. Each vessel also had a foul-smelling fishmeal plant that produced oil and meal from the remains. With a crew of ninety-five, the Seafreeze Pacific operated around the clock. Assigned to the processing deck, I was watched over by the capable John (Joachim) Schmiedtke, who later became a Vice-President of Arctic Alaska Seafoods, which at one time was one of the largest fishing companies in Alaska.

Soon after leaving the dock at Bellingham, Washington, I found myself in a large windowless room full of noisy machinery and pretty orange perch, trying hard to look dignified in my white apron, yellow rubber boots, and black hairnet. My older brother, Charles, signed on as a licensed third mate, but I was a processor. In fact, I wasn't even a full processor at first. I was a processor apprentice, a designation that landed me at the lowest pay grade on the boat. But it was a job. I was not alone. Wayne and Jerry were also not quite processors. In the factory, we were given places to stand and were entrusted with knives—sharp knives. Our knives were an integral part of processing the endless procession of fish that filed through the factory each day.

Whole fish were first fed into a green machine the size of a mini-van. Fillets emerged from the machine and landed on a conveyor belt bound for a skinning machine while the leftovers washed down a trough of water toward the stinky fishmeal plant in the stern. From the skinning machine, the fillets bumped down a roller conveyor to our waiting blades. We made them pretty by trimming the rough edges, removing bits of leftover skin, and excising the occasional flesh-burrowing worm. Although Wayne, Jerry, and I were merely apprentice processors, we were each given, along with our sharp knives, a personal fish bin. Fillets flowing from the skinning machine moved to our bins on a belt. We could either watch them convey right on past us to fall in an unsanitary pile on the factory floor, or any one of us could open his gate, collect some fillets to trim, and toss the perfected product onto a freezer-bound beltway.

Jerry was a friendly guy who had been a beautician but found that steady work interfered with his desire for drinking. He was sober for several months and was getting back on his feet. We spent much of our shift in conversation and tried to govern the flow of fillets between us in an equitable manner.

Wayne was unhappy. He was unhappy with the work, the pay, the hair net, and life in general. His work was slow and sloppy, leaving Jerry and I to pick up the slack. He avoided conversation except to interject a criticism or complaint. The irritation of his constipated work ethic and constant complaining was surpassed only by his habit of closing his bin and slipping away for cigarette breaks. During one of Wayne's departures, I opened his bin and closed Jerry's and my own. As the fish piled into Wayne's bin, I arranged them to maximize the bin's capacity. A mountain of fillets met him when he returned. He was furious. His face flushed scarlet, and he folded his fingers into tightly clenched fists held stiffly at his sides. "Who opened my bin?" he screamed.

"Umm, I did," I replied with a nervous grin.

Wayne was coming for me quickly, fists now in front. "Why?" he yelled, as he drew back his arm and coiled to strike. Would he really clobber a little kid? It sure looked that way. Before I could react, Jerry slipped around me and landed a terrific blow to Wayne's jaw. Wayne stumbled backward and collapsed unconscious on the deck. After he awakened, Wayne's breaks came to an end. He worked harder, complained less, and was friendlier. Apparently he just needed a nap.

A few hours after Wayne woke up, the fillet machine operator, Dave Slater, knocked out the skinning machine operator. He was a spindly guy with a sour disposition, thick black glasses and a green complexion who liked to be called Frenchy. Frenchy ignored Slater's repeated requests to refrain from inserting a knife into the moving blades of the skinning machine. Slater realized the possibility that the knife could be kicked out of the machine with the potential to injure someone, most likely Frenchy. In response to Frenchy's refusal to heed his request, Slater punctuated his argument with a short jab to Frenchy's jaw. Frenchy crumpled to the deck.

The Fishmeal Brigade

Trimming fillets requires little mental exertion. Some hand-eye coordination is necessary to prevent the trimming of one's own flesh, but that's about it. My hands kept busy beautifying fillets while my thoughts wandered in all directions. We worked six hours on and six hours off with fifteen-minute breaks halfway through the shift. The work was uninteresting and repetitive. But occasionally another assignment interrupted the monotony. To utilize the whole fish, a rank rendering plant converted fish waste into oil and meal. Every week or so, all the processors and all the apprentice processors conveyed fifty-pound bags of fishmeal from the meal plant in the stern to the meal storage area in the bow. There was no mechanical method of transport and no pleasant route from plant to storage. Why put a storage space at the opposite end of a ship from the production area? It was a precarious obstacle course around pipes, over pumps, through hatches, and into the forward hold. I cursed an unknown naval architect for his inefficient and uncaring design. Each of us took a bag, navigated the convoluted course, and returned for another. Except for Jake Barrell. Jake Barrell was a powerfully built Neanderthal with fiery red hair and a bushy beard. He took a bag with each arm and tossed them up on his shoulders for the trek to the bow. For hours like little ants (and one big red ant) we carried the burdensome bags until the meal plant was empty.

Mutiny on the Seafreeze

In my off time, when not sleeping or watching a sixteen-millimeter movie on the boat's projector, I spent time on the top deck watching asteroids flare into oblivion, eating grilled swiss cheese sandwiches, and pondering my place in the universe. I enjoyed my time off, and the work wasn't bad either. But when Slater became sick, everything changed. It wasn't Slater's fault. He was a decent man and my friend. In better times he served his community as a Methodist minister. A problem with alcohol led to his dismissal from the ministry and divorce from his wife. He no longer had hope for his own redemption, but plaintively counseled me to avoid making the same mistakes. I liked Slater and enjoyed his paternal regard for my future. I was frequently teased, mostly regarding my virginity. After a few playful but crude barbs had been tossed in my direction, Slater reprimanded the men. "Not one of these men are happy with who they are," he counseled. "Don't listen to them."

A month into the trip, there began to be problems with some of the men who were unused to the work, the life at sea, and the inaccessibility of some of their favorite vices. They wanted to go home. Some were desperate. I was usually the first one to show up on the factory deck for my shift. One morning, after the previous shift had finished early and left the factory empty for several hours, I discovered that all the conveyor belts had been cut. Someone apparently thought that cutting conveyors would force the termination of the trip. The ship's engineers were able to make repairs, but several hours of processing time, and wages, were lost.

Later, chips of glass were found in the crew's galley coffee maker. It was not long after that that the men stopped work and held a meeting. I sat off to one side of the galley with a couple of friends and a bowl of popcorn. "Slater is dying," they said. "And the captain refuses to take him to town." Several of the more motivated speakers stood on tables and bellowed belligerently about intolerable conditions and the length of the trip. In the absence of eloquence, they punctuated their concerns with cursing and stomping. There were a few threats of violence and some of the men brandished fire axes. Eventually, calmer heads constructed a list of demands, and a delegation was chosen to confront the captain. I accompanied the group carrying the grievances topside, not because I was unhappy with conditions on the ship, but because the captain was my father and I was interested to see how he handled the situation.

The delegation insisted on contacting the Red Cross, the Coast Guard, and their union. It was an act of mutiny, and they failed to find a sympathetic ear in any of these organizations, especially their union who threatened to expel anyone who quit. Seaplanes were called in to transport the dissenters ashore (at their expense). About half the crew left. Slater stayed. For one who had but moments to live (according to the antagonists), Slater didn't look bad. He arose from his deathbed and climbed three flights of steep metal stairs to speak with the captain. He apologized for his illness and declared his intent to remain on the boat and work as soon as he was able. "You gave me a job when I needed one," he said, "and I'm not going to let you down." Soon after, he recovered sufficiently to return to work.

Climbing the Cardboard Staircase

With half the crew now gone, overtime was not only an opportunity, but also a necessity. The two previous six-hour shifts were consolidated into one eighteen-hour shift. I was promoted to a full processor and moved to a position that was more interesting but much harder. I still wonder why Mr. Schmiedtke thought I was even capable of the job, but I did it. Fillets spilled from the blast freezer conveyor into wire baskets. My job was to dip the baskets of frozen fish into a glazing solution and dump them into boxes. I also assembled the boxes and made the glaze. A full box of fish weighed from 110 to 130 pounds. I weighed and marked each box and loaded it onto an elevator.

When I had four boxes on the elevator, I set out a bunch of baskets to catch spilling fillets, quickly pulled on a freezer suit, and climbed down an icy ladder into the freezing fish hold. I worked alone, doing a job previously assigned to two men.

I had to work fast in the freezer. Not only would my nose go numb but if I took too long, I returned topside to find frozen fillets overflowing the baskets and sliding across the deck. Stacking boxes in the freezer was the hardest part of the job. They had to be stacked from floor to ceiling in an eighteen-foot high fish hold, so I constructed stairs from boxes lower down to reach the top layers. I filled and stacked hundreds of boxes every day, often working up to twenty-one hours a day. Frequently too tired to climb all the steel stairs between the factory and my stateroom, I curled up on a pile of cardboard and slept for a few hours until the fillets started falling out of the blast freezer again.

Even in those years, a fifteen-year-old boy working twenty-one-hour shifts carrying 120-pound boxes of fish alone in the freezer of a factory trawler was a stretch of what most people would consider appropriate. But that's what I did. Often I would be sore, tired, and discouraged. I wanted to quit, but I kept working and grumbled only to myself. A few times I slipped on the icy floor of the freezer, and a big box of fish landed on my chest or legs. It hurt, but I got up again. I had a job to do and like Slater, I appreciated it.

At the Helm of America's Largest Fishing Ship

On a few nights, I was summoned to the wheelhouse to drive the boat. The deckhands were subject to union hours, and were off work when it came time to haul back the final tow of the day. The officers took their places on deck, leaving a fifteen-year old kid alone in the wheelhouse to operate the largest fishing vessel in the United States. My father hollered instructions over a small radio. "Turn twenty degrees to port. No! No! No! That's too much. Slow down. No, don't stop. Be careful, the net is going in the propeller. Speed up. Slow down. Turn the rudder hard to the right. No! No! No! Gee whiz. My right, not you're right! Don't you know nothing?"

Even though I tried to do exactly as he said, it always seemed to be the wrong thing. Yet, despite my inadequacies as a captain, we always got the net in without serious mishap. I missed my home and friends. While I was mindlessly trimming fillets, toting bags of fish meal and loading heavy boxes of fish in a ship's freezer hold, my friends were enjoying a lazy summer of fun activities. On the other hand, I was a fifteen-year-old in charge (albeit temporarily) of the largest fishing ship in the country! And I made $5 an hour and $7.50 for overtime. I couldn't really complain.

The Portuguese Arrive

Rumors of the imminent arrival of Portuguese fishermen who were experts in net mending quickly spread through the boat. Our deck crew was sadly deficient in net mending skills, and the efficiency of our trawl was rapidly declining. Most of them should have been processors. A few days later, seaplanes arrived with the rumored reinforcements. At the time, I had no idea the significance that moment held for the Bering Sea crab and trawl fleet, or inkling of the fact that I would be friends and shipmates with some of these men for many years to come. They didn't speak English and mostly kept to themselves, but they kept the nets in good repair. They were also not union members, and I no longer had to spend time in the wheelhouse that was better spent curled up on a pile of cardboard. After more than two months at sea, the long awaited time arrived when the City of Bellingham, Washington appeared on the horizon, and the end of the trip arrived. After a night of drunken revelry celebrating their return to civilization, the crew was dismissed, but I stayed on to clean up the mess.

Mothballs

On the last voyage, the Seafreeze Pacific encountered a vicious storm and sought shelter in a bay, dropping its two fifteen-hundred-pound anchors. But soon after anchoring, an engineer's mistake resulted in a flooded turbine room and the loss of all propulsion and electrical power. The boat went black. As repairs were effected, the wind shifted directions and the ship began dragging its anchors toward a rocky coast. All hands, except engineers and officers were ordered topside and issued life jackets. Preparations were underway for abandoning ship, if necessary. But before the life rafts were launched, word came from the engine room that the problems had been resolved. The engines were started and the vessel returned to fishing.

Later in the trip, my father was summoned to the engine room. An assistant engineer lay paralyzed on the deck. "How are you feeling?" he asked the man.

"Oh, terrible," the man replied. "I can't move a muscle. I am paralyzed all over."

"Perhaps," suggested my father, "you could use some rest. Why don't you go lie down in your bunk, and we will see how you feel tomorrow."

"Yes, that is what I need," replied the man as he got up and walked to his stateroom.

The company struggled with profitability issues and mothballed both of the Seafreeze ships. Pan Alaska Seafoods later purchased the Seafreeze Pacific and converted it to a crab-processing vessel (renamed the Royal Sea). The Magnuson-Stevens Act, passed by Congress in 1976, spawned a fleet of domestic trawlers harvesting pollock in the Bering Sea. Subsequently, both Seafreeze vessels were reactivated as trawlers and equipped for processing Pollock. The Seafreeze Pacific (Royal Sea) became the Katie Ann. The Seafreeze Atlantic became the Arctic Trawler and later the Seafreeze Alaska. My brother Charles Jacobsen was captain of the Arctic Trawler for over a decade, and I spent a short time in the wheelhouse as well, taking it from Seattle to Dutch Harbor for my brother.

CHAPTER 3

BACK ON THE PARAGON

Catching Dogfish

With the Seafreeze in mothballs, my father returned to running the Paragon. The crew that summer (1970) consisted of my brother Charlie, my sister Nancy (our cook), Tony Novo (one of the Portuguese fishermen from the Seafreeze Pacific), and myself. In the 1960s and early 1970s, long hours of hard work, sloppy seas and an abundance of fish characterized trawling off the West Coast of the United States. We targeted ocean perch, rockfish, black cod, ling cod, and sole. Sometimes we hauled up mostly dogfish for which there was no market at the time.

Dogfish are a small shark with sandpaper skin and two slightly venomous dorsal spines specifically evolved for impaling the extremities of deckhands. Wolf eels, skates, as well as various other fish and invertebrates—including delicious giant prawns—were also discarded or eaten. On rare occasions, a tow produced almost all dogfish.

Expanding air in the swim bladders (a bag of compressed gas found in some fish to help them float) of many fish causes the net to explode to the surface. A net full of orange perch, erupting from the green depths was always beautiful and exhilarating. But sometimes the net hung almost straight down, indicating either sole, which lack a swim bladder, or dogfish. We hoped for sole, but sometimes we got dogfish. On a fairly calm summer's day, we hauled back a heavy net that hung straight down. Dogfish filled the net to its throat. Because of its weight, an attempt to bring it aboard may result in the net snapping off or becoming stretched and mangled. We cut the web down the sides of the net to create holes and used the hydraulic net reel to carefully shake the stubborn mass of small sharks to freedom. Slimy fish slip right out of a hole in the net, but dogfish don't slide. In the past their skin was used as sandpaper. It took hours to empty the net, and we spent the remainder of the day repairing the self-inflicted wounds in the web. Other objects occasionally surfaced in the net as well. Bombs, coffins, pieces of sunken ships, and many other odds and ends laying around on the seafloor found their way to our deck.

Catching Coffins

Earlier that year, on the eve of Easter, the Paragon was fishing off the coast of Washington. In the galley late that evening, the crew discussed death and resurrection—subjects that were appropriate for the occasion, but which some of the crew considered bad luck. Olaf, in particular, was uncomfortable with talk of death on a boat. He wanted no part of the discussion.

The crew started the winches to haul in the net, and soon a bag of bright orange perch burst from the darkness behind the boat. The crew noticed an unusual metal object in the net as it swung over the bulwark. The fish were dumped out; and a metal coffin wrapped in a rusted chain, hit the deck with a thud. The chain fell off allowing the lid to slide along some slippery fish, followed by a neatly dressed, headless corpse. The eerie spectacle of a decapitated corpse convulsing from contact with the flapping fish was more than the crew could bear. Darting across the fish-filled deck, they raced to the stern where they hid behind the net reel.

It was only after a half-hour of calming, persistent persuasion that my father was able to convince the cowering crew that despite it's writhing, the body was going to leave the boat only with their assistance. They crept cautiously back to the coffin, cleaned out the fish that had fallen in, and tried to maneuver its decapitated cargo back inside. The corpse was evidently held together only by the polyester suit it was wearing, and time in the sea had weakened the suit's stitching. When Jonas tried to lift an arm with a pitchfork, the arm came off. Losing limbs did little to assuage apprehensions already approaching terror. Eventually, the cadaver was coaxed into the coffin and returned to its resting place on the sea bottom.

The fish on deck are sorted by species into compartments in the boats below deck fish hold. A deckhand works in the hold shoveling ice onto the fish as they come down. On the Paragon the bottom of the fish hold was twelve feet below the hatch coaming. Olaf was the most squeamish of the deckhands, and it was his turn to ice the fish. With visions of the dead body still fresh in his thoughts, he climbed down the ladder and went to work. When the fish were nearly all off the deck, the other fishermen decided to play a little joke on Olaf. Fred hollered down, "Hey Olaf, I found the head! I'll throw it down to you." At that point my father turned out the lights to the deck. Fred threw down a large fish with only a scant moonlight to trace its fall. It hit the slushy water at the bottom with a loud splat. Vessels well beyond the horizon must have heard Olaf's terrified cries as he shot from the black space below. He refused to re-enter the hold for the remainder of the trip.

Bow Watch

On foggy days, I was sent to the bow to watch for boats. The Paragon was built as a typical west coast halibut longliner with an aft house and raised bow. The bow carried anchor gear and a forward mast. The bow was a dangerous place, not only because heavy seas frequently swept across it, but also because the only protection against falling or being carried overboard was a small pipe rail that ran about 10" above the deck around the perimeter. When the sea was blanketed with thick fog—as it frequently was—I was sent forward to the bow to look and listen for hazards ahead. The boat had radar, but it was a vintage model salvaged from an old warship and could not always discriminate between a freighter and a fog bank.

I didn't mind bow watch when the seas were calm. I would lie on the bow and peer through the dense gray clouds at the gray expanse beyond. When the weather was rough, I pulled on my boots, gloves, and raingear, and followed the anchor chain to the stem. The cold salt spray stung my eyes and face as I struggled to see ahead. Occasionally a wave reached over the bow. I clung even tighter to the anchor chain, recoiling at the cold sea leaking to my skin. For hours I kept my post on the cold steel of the bow stem, gripping the anchor chain, and peering through the fog with salt-swollen eyes. It would be a few years before I was fit with glasses for nearsightedness. That probably explains why I would occasionally hear the low drone of distant fog horns, but never see anything but the gray haze of the Pacific Ocean's gloomy blanket.

Tony and Tuna

Tony Novo didn't believe it was possible to catch fish on the surface of the ocean, especially with a barbless hook. My father wanted to try some tuna fishing and placed a box of fishing gear on the galley table. "Make the lines about thirty feet long," he said. Tony picked up a red and white feathered tuna jig. There was no barb on the hook. He rolled it in his hand. "No fish," he announced sadly.

Tony didn't speak English well. He was from Portugal and came to America the previous year to work on the Seafreeze Pacific. Tony worked on Portuguese and German trawlers fishing in the Atlantic Ocean and the North Sea. An accomplished deckhand and expert net mender, he was an experienced fisherman with a wealth of seafaring and fishing knowledge. He raised the tuna jig for my inspection. "No fish," he repeated. "No tuna."

As the Paragon coursed through the Straight of Juan de Fuca, Tony reluctantly helped my brother and I rig the tuna gear. "No tuna," he plaintively reminded us. "No fish." Perhaps it was just as well, I thought. All of the tuna boats I had seen had hydraulic haulers on the stern to pull the fish to the boat. Our boat had no such equipment. The captain told us we had no need for haulers. "Back in the old days we never even heard of them," he said. The old days didn't seem very efficient. "No tuna," Tony knowingly assured us.

The barbless "no fish" tuna jigs were tied to wires—like long guitar strings—that led to pieces of shock-absorbing rubber tubes arranged along the stern, and along long poles extending out from both sides of the boat. Tony just shook his head. Upon arriving at the fishing grounds, the boat slowed to trolling speed. A light breeze rippled the water atop slow rolling swells. My brother and I threw the jigs over the stern while Tony sat dejectedly in the galley. It didn't take long. First one rubber tube stretched to its limit, then another and another. We started hauling the wires, hand over hand, swinging the large, sleek fish onto the deck and throwing the jig over again as fast as we could. Tony emerged from the galley in wide-eyed amazement. "One tuna!" he screamed, "ONE TUNA!" He joined in the hauling with the glee of a child at Christmas, repeatedly yelling "ONE TUNA!" as loud as he could as each fish came aboard. Each time another tuna was brought aboard, all the fish would start flapping their tails on the deck, creating a thunderous applause. We hauled frantically for fifteen or twenty minutes, and then the fish vanished as suddenly as they had come.

Tony tended the lines while my brother and I packed the fish with ice in the hold. Soon Tony's happy cry of "one tuna" sailed across the deck and we started hauling again. By the second day, Tony had done so much screaming that he could only speak in a hoarse whisper. Our hands were bleeding and blistered from pulling the thin steel lines aboard as our plastic gloves offered little protection from the sharp wire.

Our tuna trip lasted only a week, and my lacerated hands would not have tolerated much more. In the old days I imagine they wore leather gloves, with steel reinforcement perhaps. We sold most of the fish to a downtown Seattle fish buyer to cover fuel and other expenses, and kept the rest for canning at home. Trolling for tuna was an interesting and fun diversion from trawling, and a lesson for Tony, but never something we seriously pursued.

The Paragon's Demise

I was a senior in high school when the Paragon burned. It was a calm day. The boat was trawling for rockfish off the coast of Washington when smoke began billowing into the galley. The fire started in the engine room and climbed quickly up the wooden planking, eventually consuming most of the boat above the waterline before it sank. It happened quickly. Grabbing a fire extinguisher, my father dove into the smoke-filled engine room, searching for flames. But the thick black smoke was overpowering. Choking and coughing up soot, it was all he could do to climb back up the ladder. Although the fire was eating through the decks below, and the life raft had inflated upside down, my father had the presence of mind to rescue some important papers and a new pair of socks.

After righting the raft and abandoning the burning boat, the crew drifted for several hours in calm seas. Fortunately they were close to well-travelled sea-lanes. The captain of a tugboat bound for Hawaii with a barge-load of Oldsmobiles noticed the smoke and changed course to investigate. Eventually he spotted the raft, a dark, drifting dot in an expansive green seascape. Maneuvering alongside the raft, the tugboat captain exclaimed, "Captain Jacobsen! What are you doing down there?"

My father lost his boat, and I lost my summer job. A future directing traffic at the Aurora Drive-In Theater or mopping floors at the Royal Fork Buffet seemed dismal. I was seventeen, finishing high school, and needed more than a minimum wage job to pay for college. When my father asked if I wanted to go crab fishing in Alaska, I responded instantly in the affirmative. I knew nothing about fishing crab. It was still a fledgling fishery, but I thought it must be better than cleaning bedpans at the Four Freedoms Retirement Home.

CHAPTER 4

THE PACIFIC VOYAGER

North to the Bering Sea

The Pacific Voyager, a ninety-six foot steel boat built by Martinolich Shipyard in 1969, pulled out of Seattle in early June. I was hired as a half-share man, the beginning status for most crab fishermen. Fishing crews are paid a percentage of the revenues from the catch. On the Pacific Voyager that year, a full-share percentage for a deckhand was six percent of the gross sales. We wound through the inside passage, a mostly sheltered route through the islands of British Columbia and Southeast Alaska, pausing briefly in Petersburg. We then headed into the open waters of the North Pacific Ocean en route to Dutch Harbor. Kaare Ness, the captain and owner of the Pacific Voyager, was a Norwegian who spoke with a thick accent. He had a habit of asking yes or no questions and answering them himself with both a ya and a no. Kaare later partnered with Chuck Bundrant and Mike Jacobson to found Trident Seafoods, one of the largest seafood companies operating in Alaska today.

The rest of the crew was Norwegian as well, including my father who went along for a trip or two to observe crab fishing. He was considering building or buying a crab boat and entering the fishery. The other crew members were Arne Ness, the captain's son who later became a dentist, and Sigmund Andreassen the deck boss, who fished for many years as the captain of various crab boats. As the only non-Norwegian speaker, I missed out on much of the conversation. Norwegians and Americans of Norwegian heritage pioneered and, at the time, predominated crab fishing in the Bering Sea.

It was not my first time through the inside passage. I paid attention on the trip from Cape Spencer to Seattle on the Paragon when I was fourteen. I navigated some of the more difficult passages—Active Pass, Seymore Narrows, and Wrangell Narrows. Under my father's watchful eye and occasional correction I calculated the course and steered the boat through.

In favorable weather, the inside passage is an abundant feast of sight and sound. The buoy bells, gulls, and cascades of bow wash provide a soundtrack upon which emerald islands majestically beckon the adventurous spirit. But the beauty of the inside passage belies its dangers. The hazards of narrow passages are not limited to rocks, shoals, and channels. The tides that race through some areas can be ferocious and even deadly. If the tide is running against a boat, it can slow it down to a dead stop, or even force it backward. A hard charging current running the same direction as a boat can turn it sideways if the captain is not careful. This trip was pleasant. It was June and summer settled upon Southeast Alaska with its characteristic sequences of rain and shine.

Before Crab Fishing Got Crazy

The Port of Dutch Harbor is located at Unalaska, a small city in the Aleutian Islands that is consistently among the top seafood producing ports in the United States. As the Pacific Voyager entered Unalaska Bay, I was introduced to Priest Rock. A silent sentinel standing at the tip of the bay's entrance, Priest Rock became the object of my perennial final farewell promises never again to return to Dutch Harbor. And each year at my return, my faithful friend welcomed me back, saying nothing, understanding nothing; simply serving as a quiet reminder of how easily promises are preempted by expediency.

Dutch Harbor was an active military base during World War II, and in 1972 remnants of its past service were everywhere. Empty gray buildings arranged in rows filled large flat clearings. The treeless hills hosted bunkers, pillboxes, and hidden passages. Even craters from wartime bombings were evident. The Pacific Voyager's crab pots were stored in Dutch Harbor. We loaded them on the boat, making repairs to the pots as we went. My shipmates made it clear that I was a slow learner, incompetent, and would never survive the rigors of crab fishing. I was new to crab, but not to fishing. I considered their criticisms a common disparagement for half-share crewmen. I was certain none of them stacked 120-pound boxes of fish in the hold of a factory trawler twenty-one hours a day. I could do it.

Leaving Dutch Harbor with the deck stacked high with crab pots, we ran in fair weather to fishing grounds north of Unimak Island. My first duty was to pulverize half-frozen, forty-pound blocks of herring with an axe head welded vertically to a pipe. I stuffed the fragmented oily fish into perforated plastic bait jars.

Crab fishing seemed simple compared to trawling. A pot is pulled by a boom's winch onto a hydraulic platform called a launcher. A launcher does not launch the pot like NASA launches rockets, or like a gymnast catapults from a springboard. A crab pot launcher is raised at an angle above the bulwark, so the pot slides off into the sea. After the pot is launched or set, the line is thrown overboard, followed by buoys.

Pots are set in rows called strings. There is no set length or number of pots to a string. They soak (sit on the seafloor) for a day or two and are then picked up. A deckhand throws a small grappling hook to retrieve the buoys. The line is placed in a hydraulic line hauler and is coiled on deck. When the pot surfaces, a hook from an overhead picking boom is placed in the pots bridle, and the it is hoisted onto the launcher. The crab is removed. The pot is either re-baited and set back in the same place, or stacked on deck and moved to a different location.

All of our pots were steel bar frames, seven feet high by seven feet wide and three feet deep, and covered with web (netting). Web tunnels in two sides allowed crab to enter the pot. There was nothing to prevent their escape except for the difficulty of finding the exit and the allure of the bait. The Pacific Voyager used an older style of pot that had the door on top instead of in one of the sides, like pots used in the Bering Sea today. When a pot is placed on deck, the lines and buoys are stored inside it. With top loaders, instead of pulling the line out the end of the pot, the lines and buoys must be lifted out the top. Top loaders were inefficient, dangerous, and time-consuming. They would have been incredibly irritating had I known any better.

There were other differences from more modern crab boats as well. As noted, we had no hydraulic bait chopper. Equipped with the axe-head pipe, I was the bait chopper. We had no hydraulic crane. When stacking pots on deck, we were the cranes. When stacking pots on top of other pots, we were assisted by a trolley-boom. The boom lifted the pot up, and the trolley moved it fore and aft down the centerline. From there, we pushed it to where it was to be lashed in place (which could be at the edge of the boat on top of other pots). Stacking pots with a trolley-boom was a particularly perilous element of the fishery in the early days.

There were no hydraulic dogs (clamps) on our launcher. Dogs hold the pot in place while crab is being removed. Boarding seas often took a pot off the launcher and carried it across the deck. The ability to dodge pots washed from the launcher was an essential survival skill on the Pacific Voyager's deck. There was no line coiler either. All our lines were coiled by hand. Coilers came along after I was in the wheelhouse. We didn't even have a sorting table. Today crabs are emptied from the pot onto a table, where legal crab are sorted from the discards. On the Pacific Voyager crabs were dumped onto the deck, and we sorted bending over.

My first days on deck were spent getting in the way and being pushed out of the way. Crab decks are quick, and I was confused. If I did not use sufficient speed in opening my side of the crab pot door, Sigmund would rush over, forcefully plant an elbow in my chest, and have it open before I hit the deck. Despite the dangers of the deck and the abuse of the deck boss, I loved crab fishing! There were no long nights of mending nets, no wading around in a deck full of fish, no winches backlashing or wires breaking, no wolf eels to worry about, and no shoveling ice in a chilly hold. I was in awe of the deck boss, Sigmund. Small, strong and quicker than anyone I knew, he seemed to be in two places at once. He would be working on the line, and then knocking me to the deck. He coiled line like it was his servant and climbed pots like a monkey. He never pretended to like me, but eventually, he tolerated me. I became adept at working the pots, anticipating his punches, and staying on my feet.

The Pacific Voyager used 150 pots. We typically pulled only seventy-five pots each day, working around ten hours. We relaxed every evening and slept every night except for the last night of the ten-day trips when we pulled all the pots. That was before crab fishing got crazy. Later boats would haul three hundred or more pots each day, and crews regularly worked twenty-four to thirty-six hours without sleep.

Diving into a Storm

In the early days of crab fishing, the Bristol Bay red king crab season started on the first day of June and boats fished through the end of October. The season now starts October 15. I loved the moderate weather and pleasantly calm days of Bering Sea summers. Occasionally, however, a storm would blow through and make life miserable. Severe storms caused us to curtail fishing and bounce up and down until the wind subsided. It was during one of these storms that Kaare came down from the wheelhouse and asked "Jake, do you want to do some scuba diving today? Ya? No?" I mistook the question for a lame attempt at humor. "Ya, sure," I said, playing along with the preposterous proposition. I brought my diving gear just in case I had an opportunity to pick up a few extra dollars doing odd jobs in the calm protected waters of Dutch Harbor. No sane person would consider diving in the open ocean during a full-on, fifty-knot storm. When Kaare climbed the wheelhouse stairs saying, "Okay, I will tell him," it was apparent I accidentally agreed to something particularly awful.

By the time we reached the Endeavor, the wind had diminished to about forty knots, but seas were still running at around twenty-five to thirty feet in height. My shipmates inflated a rubber raft and lowered it into the water, with me inside, on the windward side of the disabled vessel. Tied to the Pacific Voyager with a long line, the now water-filled raft and I were tossed mercilessly toward the Endeavor. A line from a crab pot fouled the Endeavor's propeller, and they floundered helplessly in the violent storm. Another boat took it in tow but was unable to make headway in the rough water. Twice the towline parted and the boat was now adrift in the heavy seas. Without assistance, the Endeavor would soon be driven onto the rocky shore of Akun Island.

As the raft approached the stern of the one hundred-foot Endeavor, I felt like a fly in a flushing toilet. The stricken boat was heaving wildly up and down as the waves lifted it and rolled away. The tangled line around the prop was exposed when the stern lifted from the water. I thought the only way to safely approach was to dive below the boat—perhaps to a depth of thirty feet—and try to cut the tangle of line from below without being crushed. Could I keep up with the wind-blown boat? Was I diving into certain death? Would Kaare find me again, a tiny black speck splashing in a dark storm? With thoughts as tumultuous as the surrounding seas, I rolled from the raft and swam below the surface.

Just out of reach of the hull, I appraised the situation. About fifty wraps of five-eighths inch nylon line were wound tightly around the shaft and propeller. Loops of nylon line and a mess of corkscrewed three-quarter-inch polypropylene line were pulled close behind. When the hull approached, I frantically slashed at the line, trying hard to avoid being knocked out by the 190-ton ship. My initial attempts were entirely ineffective. The boat lurched up before I could make a single cut. It was drifting, and I swam hard to follow it.

At this point, I remembered the sage words of my father; "Don't just stand there, do something—even if it's wrong." When the boat came down again, I wrapped my arms and legs around the propeller shaft and held on. As the boat jerked upward, I almost lost my grip. My facemask was knocked to the side and filled with water, much of which I promptly inhaled. Before I could recover, the hull crashed down on my tank, jamming the valve into my head and knocking the regulator out of my mouth. I did something, and it was wrong. A fortuitous lull in the wave pattern allowed me to find my regulator and clear my mask. Surprised to be alive and still conscious, I straddled the shaft and wedged myself between it and the hull above. The position was uncomfortable, but it allowed brief periods of work on the line. Most of my energy was spent holding on and avoiding injury.

An audience of five or six sea lions observed the odd spectacle. They followed me up and down, sometimes approaching within a few feet. Unlike my experience with sea lions out of the water, these exhibited no hostility or fear. They were curious, friendly, and probably amused at the ungainly alien that created so many bubbles.

I worked about an hour before running out of air. Exhausted and shaking from cold (my quarter-inch thick Neoprene wet suit was inadequate for extended immersion in the Bering Sea), I did all I could. Most of the line was gone, but a few wraps remained under a shaft guard where I could not reach. Now on reserve air, I kicked away from the boat before the stern rose again. At the surface, I hollered to the deckhands on the Endeavor that I was done. They started their engine and engaged the gear. The propeller turned.

Some of the Endeavor's deckhands held rifles. "What's with the rifles?" I asked. They explained that they were shooting at the sea lions, thinking often obnoxious animals were menacing me. I was furious. First, they shouldn't be shooting sea lions. Second, they might have hit me! Kaare maneuvered the raft through the mountainous waves to where I could reach it. My anger toward the trigger-happy crew gave me the strength to climb in. The Endeavor was underway and its crew much relieved.

Back on the Pacific Voyager, I was shaking, weak, and barely able to walk. The other deckhands helped with my gear. I showered, sitting on the shower floor, dried, and fell exhausted into my bunk. When I awoke, I was surprised to find I had slept for twenty-four hours. I was stiff and sore. Colorful bruises decorated my body, but I felt alive. The weather was starting to subside, and soon we were fishing again.

Fired From My First Crab Job

After three months of fishing on the Pacific Voyager, Kaare went home to start the construction of another boat. Sigmund advanced to the wheelhouse, and another deckhand flew up to take his place on deck. Sigmund fired me. The same day I was booted off the Pacific Voyager, I started work at the Vita Foods crab and shrimp processing plant in Dutch Harbor. At that time, there was a shrimp fishery based out of Dutch Harbor and I was assigned to the shrimp line.

I started work separating little bits of shell from the shrimp as they tumbled from a peeling machine. From there I was moved to offloading. I operated a large pump that extracted the shrimp from the boat's hold. One of my first customers was my Uncle Harry's boat the Sonny Boy. Soon after I started, a boat lost a piece of equipment overboard. I volunteered to retrieve it. The Unalaska city engineer had a compressor for filling diving tanks and graciously refilled my bottle. Finding the sunken equipment caused the processor's management to take notice. The next day I was given a more responsible position managing the shrimp offloading operation. I received overtime hours working on the crab meat extraction line and offloading crab boats as well. Today, crab are cooked and frozen with the shell on. During those years, crab meat was extracted from the shell and formed into twenty-pound blocks.

Dick Pace was the President of Vita Foods, and we became friends. He had two black Labrador retrievers, and I frequently took his dogs on hikes around the hills of Amaknak Island. I also became friends with the madam of the local (and not so secret) house of prostitution. She worked at Vita Foods part-time, and we ate together and conversed often. For some reason, she felt comfortable shared the pain and regrets of her life with me. At the same time, she extended the offer of free services at her establishment, which I politely declined. I don't think she realized that I was only seventeen.

After three weeks working at Vita Foods, Sigmund invited me to return to the Pacific Voyager with a raise in pay. Dick Pace was disappointed at my decision to go back to fishing. He offered me a position as factory foreman. Resting his large hand on my shoulder, he said, "I am going places in this industry, and I will take you with me." But I was a fisherman and fishermen fish. I appreciated Dick's offer, and his expression of confidence, but I felt more comfortable at sea and climbed back on board the Pacific Voyager. Dick Pace did go places. He founded Unisea Seafoods, a large Dutch Harbor crab and fish processing facility, becoming an influential and respected leader in the Alaskan seafood industry. And we remained friends.

I fished another month on the Pacific Voyager and managed to keep my job until it was time to pack my seabag and head to college. A few weeks after I left the boat, the Pacific Voyager T-boned a Japanese trawler, putting a large gash in the foreign ship that almost sunk it. The weather was clear and sunny. Seas were calm with only a whisper of wind tickling its surface. Sigmund and his crew were all in the galley talking. The wheelhouse was empty. The crew of the Japanese boat was on deck mending nets. Neither of the crews were paying attention. It was an improbable accident, and fortunately, both boats remained afloat and made repairs. In December of 1985 the Pacific Voyager ran aground at Cape Pankof, on the south side of Unimak Island, broke up, and was lost.

CHAPTER 5

THE PARAGON II

The Baptism of a New Boat

I quit fishing every year during my decade on the Paragon II as a deckhand/ engineer or captain. But despite the sincerity and resolve of my resignations, brief absences spent earning bachelors and masters degrees, and missionary service in Africa, were always followed by a return to fishing.

In 1973, the Paragon II was a shiny new steel combination crab boat and trawler. At 110 feet, it was longer and wider than the Pacific Voyager and carried more pots. It had a hydraulic bait chopper, a new and welcome addition. Other than that, it was configured similarly to the Pacific Voyager, with a picking boom over a simple launcher and a long main trolley-boom stretching to the stern.

Completing and commissioning a new boat can be a challenge for its crew, and the Paragon II was no exception. We filled the fuel tanks in preparation for the long trip across the Gulf of Alaska. At the same time, we inadvertently filled the galley with fuel. The carpenters built out the staterooms and installed a berth over an open fuel tank scuttle. When the tank was full, it overflowed into the stateroom, over the 4" doorsill, and through the galley, soaking the new wood with diesel oil and filling the air with the refined fragrance of fossil fuel. Even more serious issues were still in store.

The crew consisted of my father (the captain), two Portuguese fishermen, David Leite and Arturo DeCruz, who worked with me on the Seafreeze Pacific three years previous. A high-school friend (Mark) hired on as a half-share greenhorn. I was the engineer (a deckhand also responsible for the mechanical operation of the boat). My sister Nancy came along as cook. It was exciting to be on a new and larger boat, but the job of the engineer was intimidating. I worked hard at understanding the parts and pieces of the Paragon II—what they did, how they worked, and how to fix them when they broke.

Our maiden voyage across the Gulf of Alaska was rough but uneventful - until we came to Unimak Pass. Unimak Pass is a seaway for shipping along the great circle route to Japan, and the primary passage to the Bering Sea. As we entered the pass, storm force northerly winds collided with a strong tide, creating mountainous seas. My father and I were in the wheelhouse. The boat was heavy with fuel and carried a full load of crab pots, but we made headway, riding over each approaching peak. As we slid down the back of a big roller, an enormous wall of water lifted suddenly from the sea. The wheelhouse went dark as the water engulfed the boat in a thunderous cascade.

We watched in hopeful helplessness for a glimpse of daylight, but for long minutes darkness persisted. Gazing at the black window ahead, my father plaintively observed, "Well, I guess this is it." He didn't run to the radio and broadcast a distress call. He waited. And he watched the tops of the wheelhouse windows. Soon a dark green band appeared. It spread wider and brighter as it moved down the glass. Then there was foam, and finally, light. The bow shed its frothing burden, and the Paragon II rose triumphantly from the sea, reborn and ready for the trials ahead.

The fury of Unimak Pass found us again a few weeks later. Like most crab boats, the Paragon II had a steel deck covered with a wood plank deck raised a few inches above the steel. The wood deck protects the steel and absorbs the shock of falling pots. Our wood deck, like most, was made of Apitong, an expensive but durable Philippine hardwood. Heading to Dutch Harbor with a full load of crab, the Paragon II ran sideways to the sea allowing heavy waves to pound the deck. Crashing seas dislodged our improperly fastened planks and carried most of the expensive wood decking overboard. In Dutch Harbor, we rebuilt the deck with wood we scavenged from abandoned military buildings still standing and abundant. It wasn't pretty, but it got us through the season.

The crew worked well together and fishing was good, but it was never easy. Several more boats entered the fishery that year, and competition for quota was heating up. We used more pots, caught more crab, hauled more gear and spent more hours on deck than I ever did on the Pacific Voyager. Much of the time the weather was calm and beautiful. When it wasn't, we still fished. As my father later explained, "Back then we were too dumb to know we weren't supposed to fish in rough weather."

The Dangers of the Deck

Crab fishing is dangerous work in calm weather on a stable platform, but on a rolling, pitching boat, situational awareness is essential to survival. Divine providence also helps. Mark, the greenhorn, didn't see the huge green curler until it buried the deck as he hurried aft to tie a pot. He might have been lost at sea, but as the wave carried him overboard, his waist hit a wire that ran from the rail to the boom, and he folded around it. Mark fell to the deck as the wave washed by.

Crab pots are stacked in layers on top of each other and lashed together, but setting the gear requires them to be untied. Crab boats now have cranes that go right to a pot and minimize its movement. The trolley-boom system we used then offered little control, and crab pots easily became eight hundred-pound projectiles. Crab is kept alive in flooded tanks below deck. The Paragon II had three tanks, one forward, one center and one aft. With the forward and center tanks stuffed to capacity, I started filling the aft tank while we were setting a string of pots. Mark untied a pot on top of the stack, climbed down, and was walking forward on the deck. The boat took a sudden and violent heave forward, and the eight hundred-pound pot slid off the stack smashing him into the deck. We saw it happen. Convinced my friend was dead, I ran to the stern. But where was he? He was gone! A voice from below called for help. At the moment the pot fell, Mark accidently stepped into a three-foot square hatch and was swimming in the half-full tank I was filling. He was wet but unharmed.

The same thing happened on another stormy day. David, Arturo, and I were forward, preparing a pot for setting. Mark untied a pot and climbed off the stack. The boat crested a large wave and lurched forward. But this time the tank was closed. Mark heard, he later reported, someone shout "Mark" from behind him. He turned just in time to see the falling pot and narrowly escaped being crushed. We heard nothing. Behind him was a stack of silent crab pots and miles of empty ocean.

Engine Room Issues

My first year in an engine room could have gone much worse than it did. I was not mechanically inclined. I was inexperienced, ignorant, and incompetent when it came to mechanical things. My father should have known this. I didn't work on cars—I raised guppies. I wasn't interested in engines—I grew huge tasty tomatoes and decorative wart-covered gourds.

And he wasn't much help. He did not believe anyone should be shown how to do things. People, especially me, should figure things out for themselves. So when the motor to the bait freezer compressor stopped running, he matter-of-factly told me to fix it without any instruction or hints as to how. I took it apart, saw nothing wrong, and put it back together. Surprisingly, it worked. So I learned my first rule of repair; some things just want to be taken apart and put together again.

A few weeks into the season, he asked me if I had checked the sink plugs recently. "What are sink plugs?" I asked. "Sink plugs are on the engine," he replied. "You have to check them." I took out the engine manual and browsed the index. No sink plugs. Perhaps, I thought, they were a sub-part of a part, or maybe they were known by a different name. What do they do? Why do I have to check them? What should I check them for? I didn't dare ask. I was the engineer and was supposed to know these things, or find out. Starting at the beginning of the parts book, I scanned the list of every part and piece in the engine. None of the plugs mentioned seemed to require periodic checking, and none had to do with sinking. Finally, in the short list of parts starting with "Z," I found it. I failed to account for my father's thick Norwegian accent. It was not a sink plug, but a zinc plug. I discovered that the engine was cooled by seawater and that rods of zinc were inserted into various spots on the salt water lines so corrosion chewed up the softer zinc instead of the expensive engine. Ingenious!

Checking the zinc plugs required shutting the engine down, so at the first opportunity I pulled out all the zinc plugs. They were worn, but still looked fine. Thereafter, I made it a point to check the zinc plugs at every offload. At one check the plugs were gone, worn down to mere stubs. I installed new ones. Over the next few weeks, we began using more and more plugs, until I was replacing them daily. I bought all the zinc plugs I could find in Dutch Harbor and had more sent up from Seattle. I learned to pull a plug and slip in a replacement with the engine running, leaving only a puddle of salt water as evidence that I failed to follow instructions.

A mechanic looked at the engine and quizzically scratched his $135-an-hour head. An electrician looked at it as well, testing various wires and circuits with a meter designed to find out why zinc plugs disappear at an alarming rate. He found nothing. A few days later I connected with the problem. The weather was nasty. Not wanting to shut down, I replaced the plugs with the engine running. Kneeling on the engine room floorboards, and leaning over the engine, I pulled a plug, allowing a small stream of seawater to shoot from the cooling pipe. I quickly inserted its replacement. Just as I started to get up, the boat lurched violently, and I lost my balance. Instinctively I extended my hand to catch my fall. My hand found the engine frame. Electricity surged through my body, throwing me on my back and into unconsciousness. When I awoke, I knew two additional things. First, that I had a tremendous headache, and second, that I had discovered the problem. A worn spot on a wire was contacting the engine frame. My hand landed directly on the spot. Recovering my composure, I wrapped the wire with tape. That was the end of my zinc plug problems.

Shaft Separation

In addition to my deckhand duties, the position of engineer kept me running up and down the engine room ladder, and created unique opportunities for stress and worry. I was responsible for fixing everything that broke. So my heart sank when I heard a loud clunking noise and the engine suddenly raced. I had no idea what was wrong, but I was certain I would be blamed.

The main engine on the Paragon II was a 1,125-horsepower Caterpillar model D-399. It turned a six-inch diameter stainless steel propeller shaft. A bolted coupling connected the engine to the shaft. When attaching the coupling, the shipyard apparently used the wrong bolt size. Now, in the Bering Sea hundreds of miles from a port, the bolts sheared and the shaft separated from the engine. We carried no bolts of the proper size, but I did have a welding machine and some stainless steel rod. I had a bit of experience welding from working in a refrigeration shop (on a "work for free to learn to weld" program created by my father).

At the time, I had no understanding of the potential problems welding the shaft coupling together on a rolling boat at sea could cause, or that no responsible shipyard would approve of any such procedure. Misalignment can create a host of problems including transmission failure, vibration, broken shafts, ruined bearings, flooding, and sinking. But we were drifting helplessly in the Bering Sea, and something had to be done. I managed a makeshift alignment and welded the coupling together. The fix held without complications for eight years, until maintenance required removal of the shaft and the coupling was scarfed apart.

Losing New Friends

Many of our trips were offloaded to the Northern Shell, a processing barge anchored in Herendeen Bay (on Unimak Island). In mid-September, we were next in line to offload behind an old wooden crab boat named Jarl. I met several of the Jarl's crew on the deck of the processor. We chatted for some time about boats and fishing, but mostly about school and plans for the future. They were friendly and intelligent, and it was a pleasure to have someone new to talk to. I waved goodbye to my newfound friends as the Jarl pulled away from the processor. It was September 16, 1973, and the last time anyone saw or heard from the Jarl. The tired vessel vanished with all hands and without a word.

My father was captain on the Jarl for a short time. While fishing in rough weather, the engine room started taking on water. He dove into the oily water of the flooded bilges to secure the source of the flooding. He managed to keep the boat afloat but considered it unsafe and only a matter of time before it would be lost. Sadly, he was correct.

Sinking Again

It was a week since the disappearance of the Jarl. My thoughts frequently returned to my tragically lost friends. It was decades before an appalling history of derby-style fishing in extreme weather, drug use, and sleep deprivation would combine to claim the dubious title of "deadliest" for Bering Sea crab fishing. Despite close calls, sinking was something that happened to other people, I thought. Not me. I was sleeping soundly when the alarm sirens screamed. The boat listed badly and the bow was elevating.

My father streaked past my stateroom and slipped on the steel steps of the engine room ladder, crash-landing on a bilge pump below. Pitched suddenly from sweet slumber into pandemonium, I followed behind. Through the aft hatch porthole, I saw that our stern was submerged. It was clear that we were sinking. Would we follow the Jarl? In the engine room, my bloodied father and I switched valves to pump water from the crab tanks to regain buoyancy. Normally, creating free surface in a tank decreases stability and can cause a vessel to roll over. But we were sinking by the stern and increasing buoyancy was our only alternative.

Nearing the end of our trip, with crab in each of our three holds, we were running in a following sea of twenty-five foot waves. In a following sea, the boat travels the same direction as the waves. A problem with the steering caused the vessel to suddenly veer hard to port at full speed. Heavy seas filled and captured the stern, and the boat floundered. Eventually, the sea released its grip, the boat stabilized, and the stern slowly surfaced. The Paragon II pulled through again.

The scare taught me something interesting about myself. I was able to stay calm, think clearly, and act appropriately throughout the ordeal. It was only when the predicament was past that I experienced the pallid skin and shaking of traumatic shock. This remained the case in scores of close calls throughout my career.

Fishing at Adak

When the Bristol Bay red king crab season ended, we loaded our gear and headed to the Western Aleutians for the Adak red king crab fishery, 450 miles west of Dutch Harbor. A much-anticipated fishery with a recent history of quick and lucrative fishing, it was the season everyone looked forward to. Processing ships anchored in Finger Bay, a narrow inlet jutting into Adak Island a short distance from the Adak Naval Air Station. A crab processing facility was under construction ashore.

For a time, we fished close enough to Adak that the lights of the city were visible at night. Although 2,300 miles from home (Seattle), the colorful lights were a comfort—a connection to civilization absent from the black nights and gray days of the Bering Sea.

Finger Bay was a welcome refuge from winter winds. Adorable sea otters played around the boat and relished the crab I couldn't resist tossing to them. They ate each leg while floating on their back with the remaining crab resting on their belly. When finished with one leg, they rolled completely over, detaching another appendage in the process until the entire crab was consumed. Eagles were everywhere. The road from Finger Bay to the town of Adak ran through an area used as a dump. Here the eagles were particularly populous, guarding the garbage and grabbing the occasional reckless rat. Unperturbed by our trespass, they kept a watchful post.

There were tremendous storms during the fishery that year, and I became familiar with many of the bays and shelters in the western Aleutians. My father spent several years in the area while the old Paragon was chartered to the Atomic Energy Commission during its nuclear testing at Amchitka Island. He knew it well.

The quest for crab sometimes took us to deeper waters than normal. In Bristol Bay, crab is typically fished in waters less than sixty fathoms (360 feet) deep. In some of the Adak areas, we fished as deep as 240 fathoms (1,440 feet). Fishing at this depth required more line than we could reasonably handle using the traditional method of storing line in the pots while stacking on deck. We separated the line and buoys from each pot, stacking high columns of coils forward on the deck, reattaching the line when the pot was set.

Today, boats fishing in the area use longline pot gear (not to be mistaken with longline hook gear), a more efficient method of fishing in deep water. By the end of December, when the quota was reached, I made more money in Adak than during the entire rest of the year. But that would be the last banner year for Adak red king crab.

The Crab Boom and Bust
The Paragon continued fishing crab and trawling. My brother took over as engineer/deckhand while I spent time doing volunteer work in Africa. By my return in 1976, crab boats abounded. Some boats were new construction, and some were repurposed from other marine industries and fisheries. The relaxed pace of the Pacific Voyager became an intense race. Most of the boats now had deck cranes instead of main booms. Even the Paragon II sported a new twelve-ton deck crane.

The king crab biomass was booming, and the fishery entered its golden era. The Bristol Bay red king crab quota catapulted from 8.6 million pounds in 1969 to 130 million pounds in 1980. With large quotas and hot fishing, the size of the fleet rapidly increased. 230 boats registered to fish king crab in 1980, while only 64 fished when I started in 1972. Processors held lotteries for delivery rotations. Boats worked around the clock hauling pots crammed with crab, filling their tanks in a day or two. On some trips when crab could no longer be stuffed into a tank with the pump running, we piled them on deck, pumped the water out of the tank and removed the hatch cover. Then we carefully packed each crab in the tank by hand. The money was intoxicating. In a few months, I earned more than most Americans made in a year. But the bubble soon burst.

As the 1980 season closed, we were still pulling up plugged pots of king crab, and I looked with eager anticipation toward 1981. I finished a master's degree in Anatomy and Physiology that year, and was accepted into a Ph.D. program in human anatomy at St. Louis University medical school. I needed one more lucrative year to fund my growing family during the necessary two-year absence from fishing. The next year I drew a good delivery number and set the gear where we left off the year before. Again, full pots of king crab swung across the rail to the excited shouts of the deckhands. In two days of fishing we filled the boat and headed jubilantly to Dutch Harbor.

When I returned to the gear, it was empty. My first impression was that someone ran through my pots and stole the crab. But the chatter on the radio suggested that the crab were gone. I scattered pots in search of the school I started on, but failed to find it. The Bristol Bay king crab fishery suddenly and catastrophically collapsed. Constantly pulling sparsely occupied pots, we were desperate. I found a small school of crab in a deep trench outside Port Moller that helped considerably, but the season was a disaster. The harvest dropped from 126 million pounds in 1980 to 33.5 million pounds in 1981. The next year was even worse with only three million pounds harvested. The Bristol Bay area closed in 1983. Many ideas have been advanced to explain the disastrous disappearance. Predation, trawling, poor management science, temperature changes, cannibalism, senescence, and disease are all candidates, but a definitive answer remains elusive. But Bristol Bay was not the only area in the Bering Sea with king crab, and king crab were not the only crab in the Bering Sea. Still, I failed to earn the extra money I needed for school and as earnings diminished in subsequent years, and bills accumulated at home, the opportunity passed.

CHAPTER 6

THE PELAGOS

Some Assembly Required

B uilding a new boat is both exciting and daunting. Memories of the six unpaid months of shipyard work and the shakedown problems from the Paragon II project tempered my enthusiasm over the announcement of the Pelagos. According to my father, the "skipper material" (my brother and me) in the family warranted another vessel. Like the Paragon II, the Pelagos would be a combination crab boat and trawler. But the Pelagos would be larger (131 feet) and have an aft three-level deckhouse with a tunnel for handling trawl gear through the middle of the first level. It was a creative design that easily accommodated both types of fishing.

As the 1979 king crab season opening approached, it was clear the Pelagos would not be ready. But financial imperatives mandated that ready or not, we had to go. In the final weeks, all efforts were centered on making essential systems operable, but there was simply not enough time. While my brother headed north on the Paragon II, I was stuck as the engineer on an incomplete and tardy ship. We were still in Seattle when the season started. And if that weren't enough, the price dropped from $1.01 per pound the year before to $0.87. The pressure was palpable. Fortunately, the Paragon II dropped our pots on the fishing grounds, ready for us to haul when we arrived.

The house was unfinished, with bare steel bulkheads (walls) and shower curtains for stateroom doors. Plywood boxes on the deck served as makeshift berths. The engine room was a disaster. Wiring was incomplete, piping unsecured, and machinery uninstalled. Few of the installed systems were tested adequately and some had not been tested at all. I knew the trip would be tough, but was thankfully ignorant of the trials ahead. Working day and night in the shipyard for the previous few weeks took its toll. Ragged and shaking with chills and fever, I weakly waved goodbye to my wife and infant son as the Pelagos pulled away from the dock.

Soon after leaving Seattle, I was at work in the engine room, still feverish and now coughing. Water accumulated in the bilges. I traced through the bilge system, opened the appropriate valves, and started the pump. Water showered from the engine room ceiling like a September storm. The overboard piping for the bilge system was fit up and fastened to the deckhead (ceiling), but the joints had not been welded. I rigged a hose from a bilge pump, ran it up the engine room ladder and out a hatch to the deck. That hose served as my bilge system for the rest of the season.

Hoping to correct a small starboard list, I closed the circuit breaker for the fuel transfer pump. Its start switch box blew off the bulkhead. Valves were backward. Alarm sensors were not as labeled. A hose blew off an engine. A pump on the port main engine blew a seal. There were hundreds of small problems—and a few large ones—all compounded by stormy weather.

On the third day, we lost steering, and I lacked the parts necessary to make repairs. We changed course to the closest port, King Cove, Alaska, steering by hand. Our water tasted like turpentine. The fresh water tank coating was improperly mixed and failed to harden. We tried masking the terrible taste with powdered drink mix, but it was still awful and probably poisonous. Four days into the trip, catching catnaps between catastrophes, I had not showered or even changed my crusty clothes. Hopeful for a hot, undisturbed shower, I removed an oil-soaked sweatshirt and greasy jeans. I was shocked to see shades of purple, red, and green, coloring my legs like a tie-dye tattoo. I thought the pain in my legs was from running up and down the three flights of stairs from the engine room to the wheelhouse, but it was apparently from the battering they received sliding around in the oil-coated bilges. After a shower with water from our toxic tank, I smelled like turpentine and soap. It was an improvement.

The steering was fixed in King Cove. I drained and flushed the water tank in King Cove as well, and every other time we stopped near a water hose that season. But the turpentine taste never completely left. Finally, with full steering, we headed for the fishing grounds. My flu was subsiding, and my brother reported that our gear was full of crab.

Finally Fishing

Although we were finally fishing, the problems were far from finished. The steering broke down two more times that season. The engine room flooded with fuel. Hydraulic oil leaked from dozens of defective welds. Hydraulic oil leaking from the wheelhouse steering system trickled across the wheelhouse and down to the galley where it mixed with water from the leaking pipes in the galley sink and toilet. I learned that the pump that should have served the center crab tank was plumbed to the aft tank, and that the water level alarm for the forward crab tank was actually the alarm for the aft tank. When the low fuel alarm sounded, it meant that the fuel working tank (daytank) had overfilled and was spilling into the engine room bilges. The old radar salvaged from a Washington State ferry broke. I fixed it with a rubber band. Despite the difficulties, we caught some crab and survived the season.

Finally, with the season over, we were stacking the last of our pots on board when the hydraulic pump started to sound strangely like a chainsaw. I ran to the engine room. With seemingly prescient timing, a hydraulic oil filter housing burst open as I stood before it. A stream of scalding hydraulic oil flooded my face. Oil reached under my eyelids, through my nose, and down my throat. I was unable to see and was gasping for air. In spite of my raingear, I was soaked to the skin with slippery oil. I blindly groped for the hydraulic motor stop switch and shut it down, somehow tearing both of my thumbs open in the process.

After recovery, I bandaged my thumbs, repaired the canister, changed the filter, and re-started the hydraulics. The noise was gone, and it seemed to be working normally. I foolishly tried for a turpentine shower. But as soon as I slid out of my oily sweatshirt, a hydraulic hose in the engine room blew apart. Shirtless, I ran back to the engine room, shut down the pump, and replaced the damaged hose. That was when the port main engine, covered with hydraulic oil, burst into flames. Three fire extinguishers and two hours later, I was able to break a seized crankshaft free with a long bar and re-started the engine. We retrieved the rest of our pots without further interruption.

I wired, plumbed, and welded through that inaugural season - and to the surprise of many—we made it back to Seattle. Shipyard workers were assembled at the dock when we pulled in. They formed a line to shake our hands as we stepped from the boat. "When you sailed out of here," someone said, "we were sure we would never see you again." Another three months of shipyard work was necessary to complete the Pelagos, but its plague of problems persisted for years.

CHAPTER 7

BACK ON THE PARAGON II

Out to Adak Again

After the disappointing Bristol Bay season of 1981, my father and I took the boats west to look for red crab around Adak. I was short a deckhand, as most of the experienced crewmen couldn't wait to get out of Dutch Harbor. A police officer friend had an experienced fisherman in jail and offered to release him to my custody. Cary's face was swollen, and his broken nose was bandaged to cover stitches closing wounds received in the fracas that initiated his incarceration. He was willing to trade a safe, warm, and stable cell for two months of torture in the western Aleutians.

The weather was pleasant until we reached Atka Island. In three days of hauling pots in twenty-five foot seas, we caught only nineteen crab. My father reported better fishing a day further west. But by the time I headed out, the wind had intensified to storm force; and we were running sideways in forty-foot monster seas. The crew was in their bunks when a huge wave set us over on our side. After activating the general alarm to alert the crew, I laid the throttle full open and steered hard over into the next sea. Happily, my tactic worked, and the boat righted.

The rest of the night was spent fighting my way to Semisopochnoi Island, where we anchored. When the storm subsided to a gale, we headed out and set the gear. I caught a few crab by Atka Island. But my father, frustrated by the poor fishing, arranged for both boats to go trawling, starting as soon as possible. We gathered up the gear and headed to Adak to offload at the Royal Sea—the former Seafreeze Pacific now converted to a crab processor and captained by my uncle Harry. While offloading, the wind picked up to fifty knots from the northwest. We still had fifty-one pots just a mile off the north side of Atka Island, where the seas were now enormous. We anchored, ate pizza, and watched movies for two days. A break in the wind gave us a chance to grab our remaining gear. On the north side of Atka, long thirty-foot high swells rolled in from the northwest. It was night, and snowing. It took twelve hours to stack the gear on board, and we were off to Dutch Harbor. That was November 7, 1981, the night the Aleutian Monarch, a 459-foot crab processing ship caught fire. It burned for five days, and then was towed to deep water and bombed into oblivion by the Coast Guard.

Losing Windows

Despite occasional scrapes with sinking, the Paragon II was a survivor. Overall, it handled heavy seas well, but the wheelhouse was too low and steep seas frequently punched out its windows. The first few times we lost windows, we inflated buoys in the openings. Later we carried plywood covers for each window, and we covered most of the forward windows with half-inch-thick Plexiglas that was difficult to see through.

In 1983, I took the Paragon to the Pribilof Islands red and blue king crab fishery. Later I pulled a load of golden king crab from the deep waters of the Pribilof Canyon. Earlier that year (February 14) on the same route, the Americus and Altair—both 111-foot crab boats—capsized with the loss of fourteen men. When we were four hours out of Dutch Harbor, the wind increased and the seas heightened. A few hours later we were jogging (heading into the seas with just enough speed to maintain steerage). While my cousin Jeff stood watch, the rest of us played pinochle in the galley.

Suddenly the boat seemed suspended in air. Jeff screamed unintelligibly. Seconds later a thunderous boom shook the bow and threw the ship violently to starboard. A cascade of water from the wheelhouse met me as I scurried up the ladder. Jeff was fine, but three of the port side windows were shattered, including one with a Plexiglas protector. Pieces of glass and plastic swirled in the water at our feet. The electric steering was now inoperable, so Jeff used the manual helm (the ships wheel) to bring the boat about, and put the wind on our stern. When he did, a small stream of hydraulic oil shot from the steering tank vent directly into a space heater, combusting on contact, and filling the wheelhouse with acrid smoke. One of the deckhands tried shutting off the heater and was severely shocked in the attempt. Running now with the sea on our stern, we bolted the plywood covers to the empty window frames.

According to my cousin, a huge rogue wave, much larger than surrounding seas, came from a different direction than the wind-birthed waves into which we idled. Did the Americus and Altair succumb to a similar event? Speculation of such preceded our experience that day. We mopped up, dried off, and changed our sopping clothes. Along with the electric steering, we lost most of the electronics: radars, radios, fishing electronics, and navigation. With the power disconnected, each piece of equipment was rinsed with fresh water and dried with hair dryers powered through extension cords from operable outlets in the galley below. Several blown fuses were replaced. After a few hours, the equipment was energized and tested. The autopilot switched on and held the course. The electric steering levers worked. One radar worked, but only on the twelve-mile range. One single sideband (long range) radio and two VHF (short range) radios worked. One Loran (an old, no longer used navigation and positioning instrument) worked. The Fathometer remained dark, but a small depth-indicating flasher chirped pleasantly from its position on the deckhead. The gyrocompass was dead, but the magnetic compass was fine. The surviving electronics were enough for fishing. I turned the boat back into the wind, and we made our way to the fishing grounds without further incident.

The seasons went well. In the late fall, we set out across the North Pacific, heading to Seattle for repairs. The electronics continued to operate until just a day out of Dutch Harbor when we lost the last Loran, our only electronic means of determining our location. Using old fashioned dead reckoning navigation, and with the help of passing ships, I found the Strait of Juan de Fuca (the waterway leading to the cities of Puget Sound) without difficulty.

Several years later, my brother took a crippling wave into the wheelhouse of the Paragon II. Not only did it smash out several windows, but it punched in the steel house front, shattering the interior wood dashboard and sending various items of electronics flying off the bulkheads. A new, higher wheelhouse was installed and losing windows was no longer a problem on the Paragon II.

Oil in the Crab

In 1984, vessels could choose between fishing king crab in the Bristol Bay and Adak areas, or the Pribilof Island and Dutch Harbor (western sub-district) areas. No other combinations of fisheries were permitted. I liked fishing the Pribilof king crab season, and my father preferred Adak. So the Pelagos worked Bristol Bay and Adak, and I took the Paragon II to the Pribilof Islands and Dutch Harbor areas.

I started the season finding a substantial school of red king crab hiding in a trench near the eastern boundary of the area. The first load was delivered to a processing ship anchored up by St. Paul Island. The crab in the forward tank looked great. The crab in the center tank looked excellent as well; but when the water was pumped out, an oily sheen was spread across their shells, and the smell of diesel was strong. It is common for fuel tanks to be adjacent to the crab tanks. On occasion a crack or hole will develop in the steel, causing contamination of the crab. A few sample crab from the oily tank were rinsed off and cooked. Gathered in the processor's galley, the quality control staff, the ship's superintendent and I sniffed the gills of the cooked crab. Gills are first organs to absorb oil and the primary indicator of contamination. There was no oily odor. We then tasted the meat. It was excellent. The processor agreed to purchase the crab and unloaded the tank.

I inspected the tank thoroughly for cracks or holes and found nothing. What was the source of the oil? Perhaps, I thought, there was a hairline fracture that opened only when the tank was full. During the next trip, I inspected the water flowing from the center tank many times daily. There was no hint of oil. The season closed, and we were scheduled to offload at a different processor. Pristine water flowed from the suspect tank as we pulled up to the processor to sell our catch. Again, the crab in the forward tank was removed without incident. The water pouring from the center tank was spotless. We pulled off its hatch, confident that the water was clear. But as the water was pumped from the tank, an oily sheen again appeared. My brain exploded in apoplectic disbelief. Something horrible had happened in the few seconds it took to remove the hatch cover, and I suddenly realized what it was. I collared the engineer and pulled him to the engine room to confront an unbelievable sequence of errors.

Along with opening the suction valve to the tank, the engineer also opened a clearly marked, red handled emergency suction to the engine room bilge—a valve that should only be opened to prevent catastrophic flooding of the engine room. But this one error would not have directed oily bilge into the tank. It would simply have directed the water overboard. A second wrong valve was also opened, allowing discharge water to recirculate. Opening two wrong valves sent oily engine room bilge through the crab tank!

The offloading crew walked off the boat. The superintendent was not at all interested in purchasing the crab. Pulling away from the processor, I circulated clean seawater through the tank for eight hours. There was no detectable odor in the gills. I called several nearby processors and explained the situation. No one displayed any interest in purchasing polluted product. The processor that took my first load was on the other side of St. Paul Island. The fear of losing half my season and the financial ramifications of such failure knotted my gut as I switched my radio to their frequency and made the call. It was my last chance. "Yes," the superintendent said. "We will take a look." After repeating the cook, smell, and taste test, they agreed to buy the crab. The brief exposure to oil, they concluded, was insufficient to contaminate the crab. I was elated. The decisions of a friendly superintendent averted a devastating disaster. From there, we loaded our pots on deck and headed to the Islands of Four Mountains.

The Islands of Four Mountains
The strong tidal currents that course through the passes of the western Aleutian Islands offer interesting challenges to fishermen. For much of the day, buoys that mark pots are pulled underwater by the tide. To extend our fishing time, we fashioned a wire loop to sink over the end buoy, sometimes

even while it was still submerged. Whether spotting a sunken orange ball, and then successfully lassoing it, was worth the time and effort was questionable—but we did it nonetheless. It is unnerving to watch buoys disappear as soon as a pot is set. Were the currents carrying them into deeper water, too deep for the line? Would they ever be seen again?

Most of the time the buoys surfaced at slack water, but not always. Sometimes water pressure flattened the air-filled buoys. For this reason, we also employed a Styrofoam float (referred to as a sea lion buoy because sea lions around Kodiak were frequently accused of popping air-filled floats).

My fishing partner at the time was Russ Moore who was running the North Pacific, a vessel similar to mine. When Russ bought the North Pacific, it was sunk at a dock in Dutch Harbor. He raised it and brought it back into service. We chatted incessantly on the radio. There were few other boats in the area, and the ones that came didn't stay long. The weather was gnarly, and the fishing was challenging. A captain new to the area set his gear while running into a strong current. Each pot disappeared beneath the boat. It was before GPS or coordinate converters for Loran. One had to be careful to make sure the vessel was making headway. He was stationary, not moving anywhere, and setting his pots one atop the other. I came upon the spot at slack water, an almost solid raft of buoys a hundred feet across. I pitied the deckhands that had to sort out what was certainly the biggest tangle of pots in crab fishing history. I would be surprised if they recovered half of them.

We worked hard at the Islands of Four Mountains. The weather grew increasingly nasty, and the fishing tapered off to a scratch. At the end of a particularly rough trip, I ran to Dutch Harbor to deliver. An old wooden boat delivered just before us. He caught 80,000 pounds of king crab in two weeks. We also delivered 80,000 pounds caught in two weeks. The old wooden boat spent most of the day tied to a dock in Dutch Harbor. Each day the crew left the dock, ran out a hundred feet in the flat calm waters of Captains Bay, and pulled their thirty pots. Then they returned to the dock and took the rest of the day off. We were pounded by storms, tortured by strong tides, and slept very little for the same amount of crab. I felt cheated. The Pelagos struggled as well. They caught little during the Bristol Bay season, and Adak was looking equally grim. But just before Christmas, my father found good fishing and fully loaded the boat twice before the season closed. Three weeks of excellent fishing saved the company from foreclosure.

Joint Venture Fishing

A 300-foot long Soviet trawler was tailing me. He was just off my port stern. Over the radio, I tried to communicate with the Russian captain. Beyond a few pleasantries, I spoke no Russian, and he spoke very little English. Our winch was broken. We were making repairs, but needed help. After I had tried an assortment of ways to present our predicament, the captain seemed to understand the words "broke" and "machine." "Oh, machine broke, oh, okay," he intoned in a slow, deep and now sympathetic voice.

A part on the port winch failed, and I didn't have a spare. But I knew that Soviet ships had machine shops and skilled machinists. The large rusted trawler belched some black smoke and maneuvered ahead of the Paragon II. A line with a buoy appeared behind it. My deckhands picked it up and attached the broken part. The Russians pulled it aboard. A few hours later the buoy again tumbled out of the trawlers stern ramp, and I maneuvered close to it. A newly machined part was attached. It was perfect. We reassembled the winch with the new part and set our net. Soon, fifty-five tons of Pollock were pulled from the sea and filled the net behind my boat.

It was my job to catch the fish. The Soviets bought the fish, removed the head and viscera, and froze it into blocks. It would later go to Russia, Korea, Japan, or another market. The crew removed the cod end (the detachable end of the net that contains the catch) and prepared to transfer it to our Russian friends. The Magnuson-Stevens Fisheries Conservation and Management Act of 1976 limited and eventually eliminated fishing by foreign fleets in the territorial waters of the United States. During the late 1970s and through the 1980s, joint ventures were formed between American harvesters and foreign fishing fleets. In a joint venture, foreign fishing companies purchased and processed fish caught by American boats. Both the Paragon II and the Pelagos participated in the joint venture trawl fisheries. Most often, we worked with

Korean ships, but we also delivered fish to ships from Russia, Japan, Poland, and China. Transferring fish at sea is usually not complicated, but can be unnerving for an inexperienced captain, or when heavy seas make maneuvering difficult. While making way at around six or seven knots, our Russian mothership sent a heavy hawser (a line) out its stern ramp. At the end of the hawser was a clump of several buoys and a long retrieval line with a single buoy. I pulled up just behind the mothership, and the crew picked up the buoy and hauled in the hawser.

The cod end was held in our stern ramp by a releasable pelican hook. Before transferring, the crew sewed the cod end shut and shackled it to steel transfer cables (which deckhands referred to as jewelry). The crew now shackled the hawser to the transfer cables and released the pelican hook. With the cod end being pulled behind the processor, another line and buoy bounced down the Russian's stern ramp and extended behind the boat. We picked it up. When it was secure, an empty green cod end slid down the Russian's ramp. We pulled it aboard and prepared to set the net again. It was Sunday and along with the cod end, they sent bread. I loved the special bread they baked on Sunday.

During the decade of joint ventures, I fished with foreign partners for pollock, flatfish, Atka mackerel, and cod in Alaska and hake from California to Washington. The development of a domestic factory trawler fleet, shore-based fish processing plants in Dutch Harbor and Akutan, and American fish processing ships largely supplanted foreign participation in Alaskan fishing by the late 1980s. In the early 1990s the glorious era of joint ventures ended entirely.

To California

A tough winter's pollock joint venture was behind us, and the crab season was still months away. I looked forward to time at home with family. But just two hours after tying to the dock in Seattle, I received a phone call from a joint venture company. They wanted to know if I could leave in three days. A joint venture, fishing for hake off the west coast from California to Washington, was planned with the Chinese. They needed another boat. Instead of happy moments with my family, my time was spent preparing for immediate departure: buying groceries, loading fuel, hiring the crew, and making all the preparations necessary for a two-month fishery. Most of my previous crew were willing to go, but I needed an engineer and put the word out on the docks. Ray was the only engineer that responded. Ray impressed me as being tired and slow, but he was a licensed engineer with over a decade of service in the Coast Guard, so I hired him. Leaving the Ballard Oil Company dock, I entered Seattle's Chittenden Locks allowing passage from Lake Union to Puget Sound. Once out of the locks, I called the railroad bridge operator and requested an opening. As we passed below the bridge, the main engine alarm sounded. Ray went below to assess the situation as I took the boat out of gear and steered toward a wooden barricade to starboard. We were in a narrow channel, with a shallow bank of mud on one side, the wood bulkhead on the other, a bridge behind, and small pleasure craft all around—not the place to be having engine problems. When he returned, Ray reported, "Fuel is squirting out of all the injector lines" and hollered that he would tighten them up as he disappeared down the wheelhouse ladder. His solution to what clearly was an overheating problem made no sense. I ran to the engine room and shut the engine down. It was readily apparent that the engine was too hot. Baffled by the apparent stupidity of the licensed and experienced engineer (why could he not see something so elementary and obvious?), and hoping that the engine block was not warped, I returned to the wheelhouse and told the crew to ready the anchor. But we seemed to be stationary, so I refrained from dropping it. The tide was slack and the winds were calm. We drifted very slowly out the channel. Ray explained that he had drained the coolant from the engine and had "forgotten" to refill it. It was a small detail he suddenly recalled while I wrapped the expansion tank cap with rags and released a jet of steam. As soon as it was safe to do so, I added water to the engine. It turned over and started, and seemed to be operating normally. Much relieved, I returned to the wheelhouse, and we continued out the channel, en route to California.

We met our Chinese motherships off the coast of Eureka, California. Four ships were on the fishing grounds and two more were to arrive later. Most of the other participating trawlers were there as well. Because hake is a soft and easily damaged fish, we used a smaller cod end—holding fifteen tons compared to the fifty-five, eighty or one-hundred ton bags we used for pollock. We kept busy during the day, making eight to ten tows and consistently delivering full cod ends. At night, the fish dispersed throughout the water column and towing produced nothing. Pollock, sole and all the other fish I sought over the years, could be caught day or night. But hake vanished with the setting sun. If there is a secret to catching them at night, I failed to discover it. At dawn, the school reconfigured and funneled easily into our net.

As we hauled back our first tow, the sheer pins in the port winch snapped. I was familiar with how to fix the problem and, not trusting Ray, replaced the pins myself. After delivering the cod end, I told Ray to change the hydraulic oil filters as dirty oil is the primary suspect in a case of broken shear pins. Soon after, he reported that he had changed the filters. But on the next tow the pins snapped again. Changing filters should have corrected the problem, and Ray insisted that he had done so, but he was clearly untrustworthy. I went to the engine room and pulled out the filters. They were old, dirty, and obviously had not been recently replaced.

Ray confessed that because he did not understand how dirty filters could cause the sheer pins to break, he lied about changing them. I replaced the filters, and the pins remained intact for the duration of the season. Ray may have been a fine engineer at one time, but he confessed that decades of drug use had scrambled his brain. I fired Ray at the first opportunity, sending him to Eureka on another boat; and I assumed the engineer's duties. It was not the first time I was both captain and engineer, and it would not be the last. Without the worry of Ray, and despite being both captain and engineer, the fishery was pleasant. The weather was calm and warm—a relaxing respite from the ravages of the Bering Sea winter. But there was certainly a lot of fog.

Fishing for the Chinese was a new experience. The six motherships represented three different companies, each from a different region of China. The companies hated each other, and refused to help if a boat from another company had a problem. Other than a compass and a radar, none of the boats had navigation equipment. They did not know where they were. Their inability to establish a position was a problem when we were trying to deliver a cod end in the fog. They could not see us and could not tell us which of the dozen dots on the radar was them.

Fortunately, the Paragon II had a new radar with technology that could create a slug trail behind each target, as well as display the target's position, speed, and course. Every morning, the motherships would take turns sailing in a circle. Each in turn, made a neat little "O" on my radar screen, and I would radio their position to their catcher boat. Once connected, the Chinese ship shadowed its catcher boat through the day.

An Injury Off Eureka

Serious injury and death can occur when weather conditions are overwhelming. But even in beautiful weather and calm seas, fishermen should remain attentive. Fishing just three miles off the City of Eureka, California, we were enjoying a warm sun, good fishing, and pancake-flat seas. Hauling back the net, steel cables wind tightly on a net reel. One of the deckhands inattentively rested his hand on an incoming wire and held it there until the wire wound around the reel, pinching the tips off of two fingers.

Seeing the situation, I grabbed the medical kit and ran to the deck to administer first aid. Returning to the wheelhouse to radio for medical assistance, I was surprised to see a Coast Guard Cutter a few hundred yards off my starboard bow. A helicopter was sitting on its deck. I called the cutter and it quickly deployed a skiff to pick up my injured man. A few minutes later the orange helicopter was heading to the Eureka hospital. Within an hour of his injury, my deckhand received treatment, but his fingertips could not be saved. Despite being down a deckhand and an engineer, we continued to fish. During the next few weeks, the fish moved up the coast, and we followed the school to the waters off Washington.

No More Toasters

It was a time when many in the fleet experienced monetary problems. The Paragon II was among the boats operating on financial fumes. Many were forced into bankruptcy and sold at auction for a fraction of their value. At the time, a joke circulated around the industry: When you open an account at (name of a bank), you get a free toaster or a crab boat—and they are all out of toasters. Occasionally I was in the uncomfortable position of having to flee from U.S. Marshalls.

The Paragon II was under repair in a Seattle shipyard when I received a call that the Marshall was on his way to seize the boat for unpaid financial obligations. I fired up the engine and threw the lines. With shipyard workers jumping off, crew jumping on, and hoses and welding leads jumping in all directions, we pulled away suddenly, leaving Seattle on our stern. I was later told that the Marshall entered the shipyard gate just as we cleared the dock. He might have pursued us to Dutch Harbor, but he did not.

A year later, while fishing hake off the coast of California and Oregon, we were running low on fuel. We were fishing outside of Westport, Washington, but I received word that a Marshall was waiting in Westport to seize the boat. Traveling to another port would take valuable time away from fishing. A plan was hatched to fuel in Westport, hopefully without getting caught. My fueling date and time were kept a closely guarded secret. On the appointed day, I waited outside the harbor until a watchman radioed that the Marshall had turned out the light in his hotel room.

The fuel dock was ready for me when I slipped into the harbor just before midnight. The tide was receding, and if we didn't have enough water to get out of the harbor, our trip would end with the slap of a Marshall's sticker. We were done fueling by 4:00 AM, with just enough water to plow a furrow through the harbors muddy bottom. By the time we returned to Seattle, we were caught up on late payments. For the time being, the Marshall was off our back.

As much as I enjoyed fishing hake in the calm warm weather of the California summer, I missed spending precious time with my family. I was happy when the Chinese ships sailed back to the Orient with their cargo of hake.

CHAPTER 8

RANDOM STORIES FROM THE PARAGON II

Tipping Over in the Gulf

The Paragon II had three crab tanks. When traveling, the center tank remains flooded with seawater. It trims the boat and creates a more stable ride. The other two tanks are usually dry when not crab fishing, but sometimes leaks in valves or hatch gaskets can allow water to accumulate. Crab tanks should always be full or empty. Anything in between creates a free surface effect that compromises stability and can capsize the boat.

On the maiden voyage of the Paragon II, a large amount of water leaked into the forward hold. Two portholes in the aft engine room bulkhead allowed me to see into the tank, and I checked it daily. In the forward hold, we carried food, fishing gear, and provisions for the Pacific Voyager, the boat I fished on the previous year. Four days into our trip from Seattle to Dutch Harbor, I peered through the porthole and saw a sickening sight. Boxes, cans, bottles, line, and buoys were sloshing from side to side in a frothy brown batter. I had no idea how so much water leaked into the hold, but as the engineer, I was sure it was my fault. The leak was later determined to be from a defective valve, but it did not matter, I was responsible.

On a trip across the North Pacific years later, I was captain. I instructed the engineer to check the tanks each day. "All dry," he reported. "No water, its all clear."

"Did you look into the tank?" I asked.

He assured me that he had. I was asleep when the wind started to blow and the seas grew rough. The boat suddenly lurched and rolled over onto its side. As water covered the starboard rail and the stern slid beneath the waves, the crew assembled in the wheelhouse and prepared to abandon ship. I sent the engineer below to pump the water out of the tanks that were supposed to be empty, and radioed my father who was about ten hours behind me. I gave him my position and reported the situation. "Well," he replied calmly, "you know what to do."

As our pumps discharged water from the holds, a deckhand donned a survival suit (a Neoprene suit designed to enhance survival if the boat sinks), tied a line on himself and swam out over the submerged deck to release the hook of our 12-ton deck crane. I then rotated the crane to the high side of the vessel and extended the boom to its full 56-foot length. The boat slowly righted as I adjusted the crane to maintain an even keel. Soon, the water cleared from the deck. The ventilation pipe for the potable water tank rises five feet from the deck on the starboard side, just behind the deckhouse. We were submerged to the point that the tank was contaminated with salt water and its contents were undrinkable.

Years of safe operation can lead to complacency and a false sense of confidence in a boat. The engineer explained that his reports regarding the status of the tanks relied on his previous experience. He checked the tanks before, and they were always dry. Assumptions should never take the place of observation where vessel safety is concerned. Even boats with spotless safety records can suddenly experience conditions that may precipitate a disaster.

Ice Fog

As the afternoon darkness descended upon a frozen February day, ice fog began to envelop the fleet of American trawlers and foreign factory ships involved in a joint venture fishery for yellowfin sole in the Bering Sea. Ice fog forms when moisture in the air freezes. It rarely forms at temperatures above minus twenty-five degrees Fahrenheit, and my thermometer indicated minus forty degrees Fahrenheit, where it bottomed out.

Peering through a dinner-plate size hole in the eight-inch thick ice that covered my wheelhouse, I could barely discern the black hull of the Tae Baek 29, my Korean mothership, as it slid down my starboard side. I was ready to execute an at-sea delivery of fifty-five tons of freshly caught fish, but as we prepared to execute the transfer, Captain Park informed me that the 29's winches were frozen and inoperable.

Other processing ships in the area faced similar difficulties as thickening ice fog formed in the frigid arctic air. Soon temperatures would drop to minus eighty degrees Fahrenheit. I had little time to find a buyer for my fish. Most of the boats were already heading toward Amak Island, a small rock with limited protection, but the only close refuge from northerly winter winds. No other Korean ships were able to take my fish. The Russians were frozen—you know its cold when the Russians are frozen—as were the Japanese. My last hope was with the Poles. I switched my radio to the Polish channel and pled my predicament. I was almost shocked and certainly delighted when a Polish ship responded. They were still in operation and agreed to take my fish.

The 300-foot long Polish processor was only a spot on my radar as I crept carefully closer, concerned about the risk of running over the transfer line or colliding with the much larger vessel that was steaming at six knots just a few yards ahead. But despite the ships proximity, a thick curtain of frozen fog kept it from my sight. And where was the buoy? Frantically peering through a small hole in the ice covering my window, I suddenly spotted it—a fuzzy orange specter embedded in shimmering white fog. I pulled ahead, and the crew captured the beautiful, eerie orb. They attached the bulging bag of fish, hit the pelican hook to release its cable, and watched the cod end instantly vanish behind a wall of sparkling ice crystals. It was an incredibly beautiful and frightening cod end transfer. I could hear the ship just ahead of me but never saw it. I could not even see my own bow. With the cod end away, I set course for Amak Island. The Poles winched the fifty-five-ton bag onto their stern ramp. But while their deck crew prepared for the final hoist onto the deck, the fish froze fast in their stern ramp, where it remained until the weather warmed a week later.

During the run to Amak Island, a foot of ice built up on our deck and four feet of water froze to each side. By the time we reached Amak, the anchor winch was frozen and inoperable. We pounded on the ice and ran hot water over the winch. We even tried heating it with a torch, but it would not yield. Unable to anchor, we began a routine of jogging slowly up to the island and drifting back again. Each morning we chopped a foot-thick layer of cement-like ice from our deck and sides.

My father was also behind Amak Island with the Pelagos. After removing ice one day, his crew left their axes, sledgehammers, and picks outside on the deck. When they returned, the implements were entirely encased in hard saltwater ice. After that, they let the ice build. When the weather warmed a week later, the fleet returned to fishing, but the Pelagos was forced to go to Dutch Harbor where they spent the next week chiseling through up to six feet of rock-hard ice covering the deck and sides.

The Suicidal Engineer

The fishing grounds were now covered in ice, but mild winds and warmer weather permitted the formation of long leads—green water roads that allowed access into a vast white wilderness of frozen ocean. We towed our net through the leads. Many of the motherships had icebreaker class hulls and plowed a path ahead of their more delicate catcher boats. When storms blew through, motherships blazed a trail far into the ice. Like ducklings behind their parents, we followed the big ships into the icepack and waited in the calm, cold surrounds for the storm to pass. Few could resist the temptation to visit other boats or play football on the ice. I could. It was cold.

Eventually, it became necessary to refuel, and we headed to Dutch Harbor. The weather was stormy. I stood watch through the night and made Dutch Harbor by morning. We fueled and took provisions quickly. By evening, we sailed out of Unalaska Bay and back into the tumultuous sea. Fishing was excellent, and I wanted to miss as little as possible. Again I stood watch through the night. It was my second night without sleep.

Toward morning, Brent, the engineer, came up and offered to relieve me. By this time the weather was rapidly improving. We were clear of the Unimak Pass shipping traffic, and still had several hours to run before reaching the fishing grounds. I headed for my stateroom just aft the wheelhouse. I was enjoying a deep slumber when Brent came tumbling onto the floor of my stateroom. "What's wrong?" I asked, alarmed at seeing Brent twitching and writhing on my stateroom floor.

"I'm scared," he said. I bolted from my bunk to the bridge, fearing we were seconds away from colliding with a ship or an island, or facing some other imminent calamity. But the weather was calm, the way clear, and we were on course.

"What are you afraid of?" I probed, baffled by his odd behavior.

"I'm scared I'm going to kill myself," he moaned, still contorting on the floor.

Sometimes the stress of life at sea overwhelms people. Drugs and alcohol take their toll. Regardless of the reason for Brent's behavior, he was a danger to himself and possibly his shipmates. He had to be put ashore. Another deckhand helped Brent to his stateroom and watched him, while I returned to the wheelhouse and changed course back to town. The Dutch Harbor police took Brent into protective custody. We located a replacement deckhand and once again set out for the fishing grounds.

CHAPTER 9

MORE ADVENTURES FROM THE PELAGOS

My Medevac

The Pelagos once had three captains on the boat at the same time. My brother was the acting captain, and I was on deck. I wasn't entirely happy about returning to a deck job after becoming accustomed to the comfort and better pay of the wheelhouse, but that's long been a complication of being the younger brother. Steve Hall, another crab boat captain, and my old fishing partner, was also on deck. Steve's boat, the Equinox, was wrecked on Umnak Island when a watchman misread the radar.

Steve came with us to try trawling. But our trawling joint venture was delayed, and we loaded crab pots to fish a St. Matthew Island crab season in the meantime. Expecting a short season, we labored day and night to be the top boat, driving as hard as our old bones allowed. After five days of hard physical labor and little rest, I was numb to pain and near the point of collapse.

Around 9:00 a.m., three hours before the season closure, we were stacking our gear on board. I was pushing an 800-pound pot into place when another deckhand jumped in to help. With my reactions slowed by fatigue, I failed to move my hand away from the pot quickly enough. Two of my fingers were pinched between the pot and the sharp edge of the forward net reel (usually removed for crab fishing). Pulling off my glove, I was astonished to see that two of my fingertips were missing. Blood spurted out the stubs, and I shouted, with shock-induced exaggeration, "My fingers are gone!"

I sprinted up the stack of pots, holding my wounded appendages in the air and leaving a trail of blood across the top deck and into the galley. My brother threw some medical supplies down the wheelhouse ladder as I climbed out of my raingear. He was on the radio with the Coast Guard. Sitting at the galley table, I found that my two severed fingertips were not missing after all. They were dangling from their digits by small shreds of skin. I set them in place and wrapped them in gauze bandages, securing them with some electrical tape I had in my pocket. Crab fishermen always have electrical tape in their pocket. A Coast Guard cutter was operating near the Pribilof Islands. They were heading in our direction, and we ran to meet them. We would rendezvous in ten hours.

When we contacted the cutter, the winds were calm, but a large swell rolled us around as we drifted. Strapped into a rescue litter, I was lowered over the eighteen-foot high side of the Pelagos. Two of the men lost their lines when a large swell sent the stretcher away from the boat. Now sideways, I smacked into the steel hull of the Pelagos face first, smashing my hurt hand. But I was too worried about being dropped into the cold sea below while strapped immobile in a basket to be concerned about my hand. Besides, five days of extreme physical exertion left me numb to pain. I felt nothing but a crunch when the accident occurred, and felt no pain until after I napped on the cutter. Soon the Coast Guard crew maneuvered me into their boat. In a short time I was tucked into a comfortable berth in the cutter's hospital under the constant care of a kindly corpsman called Doctor Proctor by his shipmates. We were still fourteen hours from St. Paul. My bandages were soaked in blood. Rather than disturb the large red clump of cloth and tape, the capable corpsman thought it best to add more gauze and tape. Soon my hand resembled a red-splotched white football.

Because of the amount of lost blood, Corpsman Proctor started an intravenous drip and instructed me not to sleep, fearing it would precipitate a coma. But after five days of hard work without sleep, and now lying in a warm, comfortable bed, there was little he or I could do to prevent it. I lost consciousness before he finished talking. The doctor woke me after thirty minutes, and every half-hour after that, to take my blood pressure and to ask my name to see if I was lucid. Only half-joking, I asked him to write my name down and let me sleep. But he didn't. I appreciated the fact that he surrendered his own night's sleep to care for me. The next morning the captain and others came to visit.

Everyone on the cutter was incredibly nice. They seemed pleased that they would be receiving mail in St. Paul—apparently it had been a while.

Ship to shore radio, the only communications available from sea at the time, was not always reliable, especially from the higher latitudes. My brother called his wife while my wife was at his home visiting. She overheard the formalities that indicated a ship-to-shore call and picked up another extension to eavesdrop. All she heard from my brother's call was, "Don't tell PJ, but Jake had an accident." She was frantic.

Off the coast of St. Paul Island, I was helped into the cutter's helicopter and strapped into a seat alongside two sailors. They fastened a helmet to my head that allowed me to communicate with the other helmets on the helicopter, and to listen in on radio transmissions from the ship. The door was left open in order to give me a better view. The helicopter leapt from the cutter's flight deck, and I was treated to an aerial tour of the island before landing at the St. Paul airport. A C-130 transport plane from Kodiak was waiting to take me to Anchorage. The cargo bay of the C-130 was cavernous. I felt a bit silly as the only freight. Again, a helmet allowed communications with the flight crew. There was no food or beverage service on this flight, but the concerned crew checked occasionally on my status. In Anchorage, an ambulance transported me to Providence Hospital. The doctor on call was a cardiac surgeon who, as it turned out, knew my mother. My mother was a Nurse Practitioner who spent several years running the medical clinic in Dutch Harbor and corresponded frequently with hospital staff. When the huge red bandage ball was removed, my fingertips were black. But on the advice of a plastic surgeon, the doctor carefully stitched them to their stubs and bandaged them again with new white wrappings. After a few hours of observation, I was released from the hospital and left in the reception area.

"Now what do I do?" I wondered. I had no money, no identification, filthy ratted hair, and a scraggly start of a beard. My clothes were stinky, salt-encrusted sweats worn continuously for six difficult days on deck. I didn't even have shoes. My feet were shod with sweat-soured wool socks only recently removed from nearly a week's residence in rubber boots. People sniffed, looked around, and moved to the other side of the hospital lobby.

Finding a pay phone, I called my wife collect, and she arranged a flight to Seattle. A kind nurse agreed to take me to the airport after her shift. I dozed in a chair as I waited. A ticket to Seattle was ready at the Alaska Air counter. With no identification, and looking (and smelling) the way I did, I was surprised they allowed me on the flight. Those were different times. Fortunately there were few others on the flight, and no one had to sit close to the odiferous fisherman in stinky socks.

In Seattle, three surgeries were needed on each finger. The bone fragments were strung on wires to stabilize them for healing. Today the fingers function normally, and the scar tissue in the tips has given way to softer flesh. Except on close inspection, the injury is unnoticeable. By the time the boat returned to the collect the remaining pots, the season had been closed for a day. Because of the medical emergency, they were allowed to finish hauling the gear and keep the crab. With the extra fishing time, the pots were crowded with crab. Everyone on the boat was happy, and I got to go home, albeit the hard way. I remain grateful for, but also embarrassed by, the resources directed toward saving a tired fisherman's fingers. The U.S. Coast Guard was awesome, and I will always remain indebted for their kindness and care.

Another Separated Shaft

The 1989 king crab season on the Pelagos was mercifully uneventful until a few hours before the season closure. A loud clunk, a suddenly speeding engine, and a loss of steering interrupted our gear hauling and sent me flying to the engine room. The port shaft coupling parted, and the propeller and shaft backed out against the rudder, blocking its motion (accounting for the sudden loss of steering).

Using a chain block, I pulled the shaft back into the boat and secured it. The steering worked again, but the coupling repair would be a job for a shipyard. We finished hauling gear on one engine. In Dutch Harbor, we had just three days to remove the crab gear, put on the trawl gear, and fix our shaft. The shipyard refused to weld it. "Only a fool would attempt such a thing," I was told by the yard's machinist. The boat had to be hauled out of the water and the shaft and engine aligned. It would take a week at least, and we simply didn't have the time. But I had done this before on the Paragon II, at sea, when I was eighteen. So I pulled out the welding equipment and went to work. We were trawling two days later and, fortunately, suffered no short or long-term problem from the makeshift repair.

Overboard

A winter gale swept the Bering Sea with 45-knot winds, freezing temperatures, and blinding snow squalls. I was a deckhand on the Pelagos, fishing pollock and delivering at sea to a Korean processing ship, the Tae Baek Ho. The winches strained to haul back the gear as thirty-foot seas rolled around us and occasionally collapsed on our stern. Once the trawl doors were up, the net was wound on an 8-foot wide hydraulic drum (the net reel) at the stern. Soon a fifty-five-ton bag of fish filled our stern ramp and trailed behind the boat like a big green caterpillar.

The detachable end of the net that holds the fish (called a cod end) has four rib lines that each attach to the net with a shackle. While it is disconnected for transfer to the mothership, a forward Gilson winch pulls up on a choke strap of one-inch diameter steel cable near the top of the cod end. The cod end was hanging on its choke strap, and two of the shackles on the net had been removed, when an enormous wave towered above us like a cobra rearing to strike a helpless rodent. As I searched in vain for something to grasp, it crashed on the deck and carried me off the stern. The wave also lifted the cod end further up the stern ramp, causing the twenty-pound Gilson hook to fall out and the cod end to slip back—attached now to the boat by only two of the net's shackles.

I was bobbing behind the boat, along with twenty tons of fish that escaped from the suddenly slackened cod end. I could touch the boat, but there was nothing to hold onto. As the next wave lifted the stern out of the water, two large spinning propellers emerged eight feet in front of me, and I was sucked toward them. Panicked thoughts of my wife and children coalesced to a single question: "Is this how I will die?" Through the storm came a quiet but strong and clear voice, "No, this is not your time." As the stern of the Pelagos crashed down into the sea, I was pushed back away from the propellers and away from the stern. A large sea lifted me to it's crest as the boat pulled away.

A foam-insulated deck suit helped me float, but water-filled boots and soaked winter clothing made swimming impossible. Catching the cod end was my only hope to avoid disappearing in the dense snow and mountainous seas. Paddling vigorously with my arms, and aided by a providential wave, I got close enough to the cod end to grip some chafing gear (masses of fibers that protect the cod end's bottom) and then an expansion strap. Straps are spaced along the length of the cod end to help hold its cylindrical shape. Mountainous seas and the forward progress of the boat pulled and shook the cod-end as I clenched the strap with all my strength. My father, the captain, was unaware that I was overboard.

When the crew recovered from their soaking, they spotted me behind the boat desperately clinging to the cod end. They shackled the net's other two rib lines to the cod end and pulled it up as far as they could on the net reel. Even the stern lurching into the air with the next wave—leaving me half hanging out the stern ramp—could not break my hold on that nylon strap. With some help, I was able to clamber back on board.

Flooded with adrenalin, I did my part in delivering the fish remaining in the cod end. When the mothership had our bag in their stern ramp, they sent over an empty cod end on a transfer line. We grabbed it, shackled it to our net, and started the next tow. Finally, when that was done, I went to the warm engine room, peeled off my cold, dripping clothes and gave thanks to God for the opportunity to see my family once again.

Compliment Number Four

During my years on his boats, my father gave me four compliments. In 1973, he approved of my welding of some cracked deck plating. In 1979, he said I did a good job in the engine room after the calamitous maiden voyage of the unfinished Pelagos. Another was after a rough king crab season during which I lost twenty pounds in the first week. This is the story of number four.

Throughout the 1980s the Pelagos participated in joint venture fisheries, mostly with South Koreans. For several of the years, our mothership was a six hundred-foot fish processor named the Gae Chuk Ho. The Pelagos was plagued with steering problems, and rarely did the repeated failures have the same cause. The electric steering went out as we were trawling in a storm with fifty-knot winds building forty-foot seas. Steering by hand, we hauled back a full cod end of pollock that extended from our stern ramp, and tested the strength of our tackle. The Gae Chuk Ho was steaming just ahead of us. Transferring a cod end of fish in heavy seas is dangerous enough, but without electric steering to make quick course corrections, the danger is compounded considerably.

The manual helm was in the center of the thirty-foot wide wheelhouse. From center to hard over was fifteen turns of the wheel, thirty turns side to side. With electric steering, it took about ten seconds for the rudder to travel from full port to full starboard. Steering by hand, it is not just a matter of turning a wheel. The pilot's muscles manually power a pump that sends hydraulic oil to turn the two seven-foot by five-foot steel rudders, while fighting the sea and the force of propulsion. It is an exercise that can take a tired helmsman over a minute, and next to an enormous ship, a minute is not always available.

My father manned the throttle and barked instructions from the starboard side, while I cranked the wheel from one side to the other as fast as I could. The crew picked up the transfer line, and we came alongside the massive mothership. All I could see to starboard was the monstrous black hull of the Gae Chuk Ho as the seas sucked us perilously close. Salty sweat streaming from my forehead stung my eyes, but I didn't dare free a hand to wipe it away.

Boats running close to each other are pulled closer by suction. A dropping wave amplifies the effect. Rising seas push them apart. I frantically steered away from the ship, and then back toward it as the seas rose and fell. For what seemed like forever, I worked the wheel for all I was worth. The pitch and volume of my father's voice was terrifying when the Pelagos's starboard boom passed within inches of the Gae Chuk Ho's steel side. I spun the spokes even faster. Finally, the cod end was away, and we were free.

Shaking and growing faint, I wobbled down the wheelhouse ladder and fell into my bunk for a few minutes of rest and recovery. When I returned topside, my father said, "There are very few men in this world who could do what you just did." That was compliment number four, and the best one of all. I went to the engine room and had the steering operational within a few hours.

Fire in the Engine Room

In the early 1980s, a Bering Sea trawlers most significant fishery was not in the Bering Sea. It was the Shelikof Strait pollock joint venture. Shelikof Strait is an angry body of water separating Kodiak Island from the Alaskan Peninsula. Later, the pollock fishery at Bogoslof Island, which is in the Bering Sea, took precedence. The fish in both these areas congregate for breeding, and catcher boats and processors hovered over them in a busy tangle of unsupervised traffic. Paying attention was imperative. Normally, there was a standardized towing direction. The captain of a boat trawling across traffic was castigated, but some did it to access better fishing.

Occasionally boats towing too close to each other tangled their gear—something I had never seen in the Bering Sea. While passing an oncoming boat, my starboard door caught their third-wire cable and snapped it off. Most boats at the time used a coaxial cable to connect the wheelhouse to a transducer that rode in a pouch on the net's head rope. The transducer relayed an electronic representation of the net's opening and the fish flowing through it. I was embarrassed, but the other captain was gracious and took it in stride.

The cod ends we used held fifty-five tons of fish, and we typically delivered four full bags to our Korean motherships each day. When the pollock roe ripened, it was not unusual to catch eight bags. The few intense weeks of roe fishing provided our primary income for the year. There were times when fish were so concentrated that we towed only two or three minutes, just long enough to spread the doors and haul back. The competition for delivery spots during this time was intense. So when the Pelagos caught fire with two weeks of the roe fishery remaining, the other boats in our group saw dollar signs.

A quarter–inch diameter hose on the high-pressure hydraulic pump burst, filling the engine room with a fine mist of oil and coating every surface within seconds. The hot exhaust lines from the two main engines and the operating generator engine ignited the oil. Great billows of black smoke surged from the engine room vents and snaked up the ladders to the wheelhouse. I grabbed a fire extinguisher and descended the engine room ladder into an inferno. Balls of flaming oil and globs of burning plastic rained from the overhead as I shut down the engines. My soft contact lenses crinkled into corn flakes, and flaming oil balls ignited my clothing.

Orange demons danced in the darkness of the smoke and fire infested space. Flames just extinguished seemed to reignite when I turned my back. By the time the blaze was controlled, a dozen exhausted extinguishers lie in a pile on deck. I coughed up black soot for the next two days. The boat had a fixed fire extinguishing system. I could have pulled a lever, and the space would flood with carbon dioxide. But that would be a last resort and our season would have been over. I couldn't afford to stop fishing. Clouds of smoke continued as we cut smoldering oil-soaked insulation from the exhaust stacks and piled it on deck.

Now the extent of the damage could be assessed. Oily soot covered every surface. Runs of plastic covered electrical wiring along the engine room deck-head (ceiling) were fused into a solid mass. I opened all the circuit breakers, changed the air filter on an auxiliary engine and started it. Then testing each circuit, I determined what worked and what did not. The main engines started and ran. The engine control lines had been spared. The steering was out, but I ran a wire from the steering solenoid switch to the wheelhouse and hooked up a steering lever. I didn't have automatic steering, but what I had was enough to keep fishing. Remarkably, everything essential still worked or could be repaired. Enough worked to enable us to keep fishing.

With smoke from smoldering oil still pouring out the engine room vents, we set the net. It took four hours to get back in action and we lost only one delivery opportunity. For the next two weeks a twenty-four-hour fire watch was kept in the engine room, consisting of a deckhand laying on the engine room floorboards (where the air was less smoky) with a garden hose to squirt out the occasional flare-ups.

Locked in the Cooler

Another very congested pollock trawl fishery took place around Bogoslof Island, north of Dutch Harbor. Bogoslof Island is the visible tip of a massive submerged volcano that emerges from the seabed six thousand feet below. The area is geologically active. Fishermen refer to the area around the island as the Bogoslof Triangle because of rogue wave activity in the area. It was while transiting the triangle that the Americus and Altair capsized with the loss of all hands, and where I lost windows on both the Paragon II and the Pacific Sun.

Each winter for a few years, a formidable fleet of American trawlers and foreign motherships bore down on a massive school of spawning pollock. The motherships were primarily interested in the valuable pollock roe, and fishing was intense when the roe was ripe. My father was on the boat. By this time he was old and worn out, so when we were both on board, we shared responsibilities in the wheelhouse.

Towing the net one night while the rest of the crew slept, my father went forward to find an apple. Produce was kept in a refrigerated locker in the bow. To get there my father descended two flights of stairs, crossed the open deck, and entered the insulated locker. As he looked through the box for the perfect apple, the boat took a roll and the cooler door slammed shut.

When the door was new, an escape mechanism allowed the door to be opened from the inside. It had fallen out years before. He was trapped inside the locker while towing a net through a heavily congested fleet of trawlers and motherships. Kicking the door didn't help. There was nothing in the locker to use to poke, pry, or hammer with and there was no other way to alert the crew. Plus it was cold. Finally, aided by adrenalin, he hoisted a fifty-pound sack of potatoes to his shoulder and ran the eight-foot length of the cooler, slamming his weight against the door. It seemed to budge a bit. He tried again and again. Finally, the latch snapped. He injured his shoulder, but he and the apple were finally free. When he reached the wheelhouse, the radio was ablaze with calls from concerned captains, but collision was avoided. The next day we ate mashed potatoes.

Losing Steering Again

Despite years of mechanical headaches, fires, and flooding, I appreciated the Pelagos for its stability and handling in heavy seas. I was able to safely continue fishing in storms that sunk other boats. Difficulties with the steering system were among the things I did not appreciate about the boat. While fishing snow crab one year, I lost steering. Both electric and manual hydraulics were inoperable, and I did not have parts or tools on board to fix the problem at sea. The boat was almost full of crab, so I chained the rudders to center position. Using the bow thruster and twin propellers, I continued to haul pots. Fishing without rudders was slow and frustrating at times. When the weather report called for strong winds, I ran for Dutch Harbor.

While en route to Dutch Harbor, the wind increased on our starboard stern quarter to a steady forty-knots with higher gusts. Seas were twenty-feet high. I was able to hold a course using engine speed, with occasional corrections from the bow thruster. The course line was not pretty, but we made it to Dutch Harbor without having to call for a tug. By the time we reached town the storm had passed. Light variable winds wafted softly through the bay. I was able to maneuver against the dock without difficulty.

CHAPTER 10

THE NORTHERN ENTERPRISE

Longlining Pots

During the summer of 1990, I spent a few months fishing golden king crab in the western Aleutians on the Northern Enterprise. Most crab fishing is done with single pots—meaning that each pot is set and hauled separately. Each pot has a line with buoys fastened to the end. In addition to fishing with single pots, the Northern Enterprise was also configured for longlining pots, where a single line attaches to many pots. It is illegal to long-line crab pots in most areas of the Bering Sea, but the practice is permitted for fishing golden king crab in the western Aleutians.

When setting longline gear, pots are baited and attached to a groundline. The end buoys are thrown overboard as the boat steams ahead at full speed. The first pot may need a shove out the stern, but the rest slam to the deck and fly quickly into the sea. Providing the crew made no mistakes, pots are pulled out the open stern in the proper order. If the pots are hooked to the ground-line incorrectly, an impressive jumble of tangled pots may be pulled off the stern together. Once setting starts, there is no way to stop.

Hauling back is similar to single-pot fishing. It involves pulling in the buoys and groundline; and as each pot surfaces, it is lifted by the picking boom (or a crane), unhooked from the groundline and set in the launcher. When the crab is removed the pots are stacked on deck. The captain must keep the boat moving down the line as the pots are brought aboard. It is usually not difficult but demands attention. With longline gear, pots can be hauled faster than with single-pot gear.

Golden king crab tend to be more spread out on the seafloor, so boats have to be able to haul a lot of pots in a day to make it commercially viable. This is possible with longlining, and makes it the preferred method of fishing for golden king crab. Many of the golden king crab fishing areas experience strong tides that pull buoys underwater. The boats use radio beacons that send a signal to the wheelhouse, telling the captain that the buoys have surfaced and are ready for retrieval. On the Northern Enterprise, before we set a single pot, a deckhand stuck his hand in the hydraulic bait chopper, and it took off his thumb. We were a short distance from the tiny town of Nikolski, so he received medical attention within a few hours. My time on the Northern Enterprise was brief, as I was just filling in for a few months while the Pelagos was in the shipyard, but the experience longlining pots would prove valuable in the future.

CHAPTER 11

THE GULF WIND

Splitting the Pelagos

The Pelagos was sold to Arctic Alaska Fisheries late in 1989, and they kept me on to run it for the 1990 snow crab season. I had an interesting crew that season. All were ex-convicts, but all were excellent crewmembers and a pleasure to have on the boat. They followed orders explicitly and never caused problems.

Arctic Alaska planned to lengthen the Pelagos by thirty feet, and add a crab processing line, with all the additional equipment and facilities necessary for operating and manning a vessel that catches and processes crab at sea. They hired me as their shipyard representative.

The 131-foot boat was hauled out on a drydock. Several wheeled dollies were placed beneath it and jacked up to lift the boat above the dry dock's blocks. Three tractors pulled the boat off the dock and into a work area. It took a few weeks to cut the boat in half just forward of the wheelhouse. It was then pulled apart, and a thirty-foot pre-built section was inserted in the middle.

The shipyard installed additional engines, pumps, hydraulic equipment, and other machinery. The upper deck was extended aft, and a new galley and crew's quarters were added. The enclosed forepeak was extended down the port side, and a processing line installed in the new space. The three flooded holds became a single insulated freezer hold. Six months after it entered the shipyard, it sailed out with a new length, a new look, and a new name - the Gulf Wind.

Because I was unfamiliar with crab processing and running a catcher-processor, I went as mate for the first season—which I hated— and later as captain. On most crab boats, the crab are kept alive in flooded holds, commonly referred to as tanks. They are integral with the ship and not removable. Crabs from catcher-only boats are delivered to a shore side processing facility where they are cooked and prepared for market, usually by freezing. Catcher-processors have larger crews that catch, cook, freeze, and package the crab at sea. They are capable of twenty-four-hour operation.

The Gulf Wind carried twenty-one people: captain, mate, engineer, federal fisheries observer, cook, six deckhands, and ten processors. For deckhands and processors, a work shift was eighteen hours. While this may sound like a long work shift, catcher boat crews, by comparison, often worked twenty to twenty-four hours a day. Sometimes they worked two or more days without sleep.

Lingerie Procurement

I designed the Gulf Wind's galley. The naval architect assigned to the task submitted a drawing, but it was overly complex and wasted precious space. I created a small paper model, and I moved things around until they all fit nicely. And that was how it was built.

When I took over as captain, the company sent us a new cook. She was an attractive young lady from Kodiak. The boat gained some notoriety after she ordered underwear from the Victoria's Secret catalog over ship-to-shore radio, which anyone tuned to the frequency could hear. It didn't take long before boats throughout the fleet were tuning in to KMI, the ship-to-shore channel. A friend called on the VHF-band radio. "Hey Jake, switch over to KMI, some girl is ordering underwear from Victoria's Secret." "I know," I said, chagrined. "She is standing right next to me." It doesn't take much to amuse men at sea.

Cauliflower

The galley called. The cook reported that cauliflower was emerging from the galley deck drains, and that water was no longer draining down the sink. "Did you put cauliflower down the drain?" I asked.

"No" she said. "We don't have any cauliflower. I don't know how it got in there."

The engineer was busy with important things, so I went to take a look. It was not cauliflower. "You have been pouring grease down the drain," I noted.

"Yes," she admitted, "is that bad?"

"Well, it plugs up the drain and eventually blossoms out the strainer looking amazingly like little bunches of cauliflower." She promised to thereafter put the old grease in the garbage.

Travelling Appliances

One day the washer and dryer went for a walk. They were installed with the dryer atop the washer, just outside the galley entrance. During a rough storm, they pulled away from the wall, broke their hoses, pulled their plugs, and danced across the deck until they found the staircase to the main deck. They tumbled to the bottom of the stairwell making a terrible clatter heard by none of the sleeping crew. But I heard it. I called a detail to clean up the water and clear the stairwell. And surprisingly, after being reinstalled, the appliances still worked.

CHAPTER 12

THE SOUTHERN WIND

Rotating Captains

December of 1990 was the last time I ran the Pelagos/Gulf Wind. I accepted a more attractive offer on another Arctic Alaska crab catcher-processor, the Southern Wind. It was a smaller boat with the same size crew. Corky was the captain. I knew his father from almost twenty years earlier when he was superintendent at the Vita Foods plant. We agreed to start the season together, sharing responsibilities and pay. After a month we began a monthly rotation.

I liked the idea of rotation and responsibility sharing. Being captain carries a demanding commitment to the boat. Working for my father, I could come or go, but sometimes I had to take a deck job. I always loathed the long periods away from loved ones. Besides missing my wife, I had five children who were fatherless for much of the year. A sixth child came later. The decision to fish or not to fish was, for me, always an uncomfortable choice between being with my family or providing for them, so the rotation idea seemed like a good compromise.

The core deckhands were experienced men who had known each other since high school, and had fished together for several years. The processors were all new and most had never been to sea under any conditions. Jim (nicknamed Buddha) was the deck boss. A stocky man with tree-trunk arms, he made sure the deck and the processors worked to capacity. The deck crew understood clearly that they only made money on crab that went into the freezer. When the processors lagged behind, they hurried into the factory and caught them up. When fishing was good, everybody helped process, including the captain.

Processing Crab

There are few variations of how crab is processed, whether it's done in a large shore-based building, a floating processing ship, or in a small steel shelter on a fishing boat. The deck crew sorts legal size male crab into a hopper. On the other side of the hopper, butchers pull out a crab and place it belly first on a dull vertical blade. Leaning into it with their body, they split the crab in half, removing the top shell at the same time. The shell and viscera fall into a flume leading to a grinder before being swept overboard. The butcher is left with a section (four legs and a claw) in each hand. A rotating drum fit with short blunt blades (for king crab) or brushes (for snow crab) removes the gills from each section. Gill-free sections are dropped onto a belt that runs to a packing table.

Packers neatly arrange the sections in a wire basket. Baskets can be different sizes, but the Southern Wind used baskets with a sixty-pound capacity. An overhead trolley hoist lifts a group of six packed baskets and lowers them into a boiling cauldron. After cooking, they go successively into a cooling tank, a refrigerated pre-chiller, a brine or blast freezer, and a glaze tank. The wire baskets are broken down. Frozen blocks of crab sections are covered with plastic, boxed, labeled, and stacked in the freezer.

Processor Problems

The processing area on the Southern Wind was cramped, cold, and wet. In bad weather, it was dangerous as well. It was forward on the deck, the area that is subject to the more violent and extreme movement. Heavy baskets of crab transported on an overhead rail could clobber an inattentive worker. As the boat rolled, boiling water spouted from the cooker. Sometimes even carefully wedged workers were thrown from their stations, and slow reactions were punished with bangs and bruises. None of the processors were accustomed to working strenuous eighteen-hour shifts in cold, miserable conditions. Tempers flared, and fighting was frequent.

Two medical conditions are common to crab processors: repetitive motion injury to the carpal tunnel and crab asthma. Butchering crab is especially aggravating to the carpal tunnel, and the steam from the cooker precipitated an asthmatic response in several of the processors. We carried a large supply of wrist braces and asthma inhalers, but they went fast. Some of the more innovative processors made their own devices for stabilizing their wrists. Some wore a rag over their face to minimize inhalation of asthma-aggravating steam. Conditions were too tough for most of the processors, and by the end of the first ten-day trip, they all quit except one.

Processors, like everyone else on board, were paid a percentage of the catch. But at the end of the first trip, despite making a months worth of in-shore wages in a week, money did not matter. The sad group of dispirited processors was ferried to St. George Island and a fresh crop brought aboard. This next group of processors fared better. At the end of the second trip, only half quit. By the end of the first month, a stable group of processors formed, although occasionally one or two would have a reason to leave. The ones that remained possessed inspiring determination and tenacity. They were there to make money and had little tolerance for slackers, who were encouraged by the threat of beatings to get better or get off the boat.

Of course, I never condoned violence. Eventually I imposed a $500 fine for fighting or otherwise physically intimidating another person. The fighting stopped, but a number of processors received black eyes and fat lips from inattentively walking into walls. A plump Pacific Islander lasted less than a day. We picked him up at St. George Island and were hauling gear two hours later. After an hour in the factory, he reported to the wheelhouse. "Do you have any medicine for cold feet?" he asked.

"Medicine for cold feet," I replied, "is called socks. Put on some socks." After another hour in the factory, he again came to the wheelhouse and informed me that he was done. He quit. Since we were still close to St. George Island, I ran back to the bay, and the deckhands took him ashore in the skiff. They may have roughed him up a bit in the process. They never confessed, but I heard rumors.

The Green Dot

One of the new processors claimed to have been a Navy Seal, as well as a Green Beret. He left military service but was asked to serve as a Special Forces consultant for the Desert Storm military effort to free Kuwait. Instead, he told us, he decided to become a processor on a Bering Sea crab boat. He professed an exhaustive range of multidisciplinary talent, including several forms of martial arts and underwater welding. No one believed his stories. As long as he did his job, we didn't care about his fantasy life as a war hero.

When he failed to show up for a shift one morning, I found him in his bunk. "Why are you not at work," I inquired.

"I have a green dot," he replied.

"Where is the green dot?" I asked.

"I have a green dot in my eye," he responded.

I examined the indicated eye but found no green dot. "Can you work with a green dot?" I wondered.

"Yes, I think so," he replied.

"Okay, work this shift and if the green dot is still there afterward, come and see me." He went to work and never mentioned the green dot again. Despite their personal idiosyncrasies and the amazing green dot guy, the processors matured into a tough and determined group that I would have been proud to pit against any other crab factory crew in the Bering Sea.

Greg's Stabbing

After the first month of fishing on the Southern Wind, I took a month off. When I came back, Corky left. He was experiencing some medical issues and did not return that season, leaving the last four months for me. Greg was a small but energetic, courageous, and dedicated deckhand. While some fishermen (like me) fish to live, others live to fish. That was Greg. He seemed to love it. But even the most competent deckhands can be involved in accidents.

Just after setting a pot, a sea came over the rail, and Greg's leg was caught in a bight of the pot's rapidly exiting line. Realizing he was in danger of being pulled overboard, Greg slashed at the line with his knife. But instead of cutting the line, he buried the blade into his calf. Finally, he was able to free himself of the line and continued to work. A short time later, Tommy noticed blood pouring over the top of Greg's boot. At the insistence of the other deckhands, Greg reluctantly came to the wheelhouse for medical attention. The puncture wound was about three-quarters of an inch long. There was no way to tell how deep it was. I disinfected the area, applied a butterfly closure, and covered the wound with antibiotic ointment and a bandage. I also started Greg on oral antibiotics.

Despite instructions to remain in his bunk with his leg elevated, Greg suited up and spent the remainder of his shift on deck. The next day Tommy came to the wheelhouse. "Greg can't get his boot on," he said, "and there are red lines running up his leg." Greg was angry when I headed to St. Paul to drop him off. He had no desire to go home. But with a serious infection, I could not risk having him so far from competent medical attention. After a two-week recovery he was released by the doctor and returned to the boat, happy to be back.

Ice Fishing

The winter was cold. By March, sea ice covered the best fishing areas, but the ice was spread out, with long leads penetrating the front for miles. I put most of the gear in a safe place and with a small load of pots, ventured into the ice pack. I set a string of ten pots five miles behind the ice edge. Five hours later, I checked a pot. It was full. We fired up the factory and went to work. I continued to fish with just a few pots. Typically, I set ten pots and would find eight or nine back again, stuffed with large snow crab. Then while the boat drifted with the ice pack, everyone butchered, cooked, froze and packaged the crab as fast as we could.

Every catcher-processor's factory was equipped with a powerful sound system, and the Southern Wind was no exception. Music constantly blared over the normal noise of the engines and machinery. The musical preference of the processors was AC/DC, Guns N' Roses, Whitesnake, Van Halen, ZZ Top, and Metallica. Volume seemed to inspire speed. I learned to appreciate an unfamiliar genre, although toward the end of the season, hearing "Highway to Hell" for the fortieth time grew tiresome.

It took four hours to process what we could catch in an hour; so most of the time was spent drifting in the quiet field of cold white pancakes. In a few days, the boat was full, and we plowed through the frozen sea to open water and found a freighter for offloading.

Aggressive fishing in heavy sea ice took its toll on the boat. The bow was crumpled and cracked. I asked the green dot guy to weld up a long leaky crack below the waterline, since he professed expertise in underwater welding. After an assortment of excuses and a failed attempt to strike an arc, he blamed the equipment and returned to packing crab. The engineer completed the task.

The Spring Thaw

In April the ice started to recede rapidly, and the crab raced north to keep up with it. Each day I pushed five or six miles up into the ice to set the gear, now using all my remaining pots, to keep pace with the crab. When I came back to haul them, the ice would be gone. The tactic was productive for a time, but the crab spread out and became harder to find.

The weather was calm but foggy, and the pervasive darkness of the Arctic winter rapidly gave way to lengthening daylight. But the boat was dying. First, the port rudder fell off. With a snap and a clunk, it vanished forever into the darkness below. Since the boat was built with two propellers and two rudders, I still had another rudder to steer with. During the next offload at St. Paul Island, a diver determined that the bolts holding the rudder to its shaft had loosened and sheared. The starboard rudder, he reported, was hanging on by only a few remaining bolts. The diver was able to secure the remaining rudder, tightening its bolts and installing others. Maneuvering with only the starboard rudder was not particularly challenging in the calm weather of spring.

Dying Engines

The Southern Wind had three generator engines. A small domestic generator had not been operable since I came on board. The two working generators had not been rebuilt for some time, and we wore them ragged. The port generator caught fire, warping the head. The engine was unusable. It started and ran, but even with a new gasket, coolant flowed freely from under the head. The starboard generator was sick. Eventually, we lacked the electricity to fish and process at the same time. We fished until we filled the hopper; and then we shut down the fishing hydraulics and sodium lights, and fired up the factory. When the crab was in the freezer, we closed down the factory and fished again. It was frustrating.

The company pressured me to fish the remaining two weeks of the season, but our last generator was getting weaker by the day. The engineer was a good old boy from the offshore oil industry in the Gulf of Mexico. He knew engines, but lacked the parts and tools to rebuild them at sea. It was clear to both of us that our only remaining generator would not last another two weeks. I headed to Dutch Harbor. Within a few hours of offloading our crab, the starboard generator coughed its last gasp and fell silent. The boat went dark.

When the small domestic generator set was repaired, we set out across the North Pacific bound for Seattle. But two days out, the starboard main engine threw a rod through its block. I ran to the engine room along with the mate and engineer to find the engine in flames. After the fire had been extinguished, the mate pulled the cover off the smoldering air filter. A wall of fire flared up between us, and I thought he was engulfed in the bright flash of orange flame. But it disappeared as suddenly as it came. No one was injured but the engine, and it was dead.

Now, with a rudderless engine on one side and an engineless rudder on the other side, I had to decide if I should try for Seattle—six days away—or head back to Dutch Harbor. I did the prudent thing and set course back to Dutch Harbor. The wind was on our starboard stern at about thirty knots and holding a course was difficult. I was not confident in my ability to navigate the broken boat safely through the traffic and tides of Unimak Pass so I arranged for a tug to tow us into town.

Under Tow

Most of the crew flew out of Dutch Harbor. I kept a mate, engineer, deck-hand, and cook on board. One of the larger Arctic Alaska crab boats was assigned to pull us to Seattle. We assisted the tow with our working propulsion engine, but on the fourth day of the trip, it died as well. The Southern Wind arrived in Seattle beaten, battered, and with only one small engine operating. I lost half of the pots (almost two hundred), caused extensive damage to the bow, and had to be towed to the shipyard. Checking in at the Arctic Alaska office, I expected a cold reception and possibly a termination notice.

But company president Francis Miller could not have been happier. Of the seven crab catcher-processors operated by Arctic Alaska, we were the smallest, but also the least expensive to operate. We came in fourth for the quantity of crab caught, but we were the most profitable boat. He explained that the Arctic Alaska fleet doubled their typical percentage of the total harvest, and the Southern Wind's production was a big part of it. No one asked how many pots I lost. Instead the question was "How many pots do you need for the next season?" Francis also said, "We are building a two-hundred foot crab boat in Louisiana, and it has your name on it." But a few weeks later the project was canceled. I was offered the 180-foot-long Glacier Enterprise instead. But a few weeks after that, they decided to send the Glacier to fish golden king crab in Adak and they hired another captain with more golden king crab experience to run it. I would have to stay on the Southern Wind.

Leaving Arctic Alaska

The Southern Wind received a new, reinforced bow and all of the engines were rebuilt. While this was going on, I enjoyed the company of my family at Yellowstone Park and never gave the boat a thought. A company port engineer was responsible for overseeing the repairs. Returning to the boat a week before the scheduled departure, I found it was a mess. I was happy to have operable engines and a stronger bow, but many other important items needing repair had not been addressed. With the crew on board, we tried to do in a week what had been neglected for months. I implored the fleet manager to remove the incompetent port engineer from my boat. He refused. Then, while the boat was loading fuel, the port engineer ordered a worker to move some hydraulic hoses, taking him from his assigned post watching a fuel vent for overflowing oil. I was furious. As a licensed master and the party responsible for preventing oil spills, I could not tolerate usurpation of my authority and removal of a fueling attendant.

I called the fleet manager and presented an ultimatum. Either he would remove the port engineer from the Southern Wind, or I would remove myself from the boat and find another job. The fleet manager again refused to take the port engineer off the project. I left a written statement with the oil dock supervisor stating that I was no longer responsible for fueling the vessel, nor was I associated with the vessel in any way. Then I went a few miles down the street and within the hour had a job working with a long-time friend on another crab catcher-processor.

At 2:00 a.m. I received a call from the fleet manager. Under the direction of the port engineer, the crew had spent several hours cleaning up a significant fuel spill. He said, "We are ready for you to move the boat to Fishermen's Terminal."

"I told you," I replied, a bit miffed at having been awakened, "if you would not take the port engineer off the boat, I was leaving. You did not. Now I am gone. I already have another job."

"But I never thought you would actually go through with it," he said. A fine was issued for the fuel spill. I was pleased for having the foresight to remove myself from responsibility.

CHAPTER 13

THE EVENING STAR

The Big Blue Bus

The Evening Star was an oilrig supply vessel converted to a crab catcher-processor by Icicle Seafoods. Don, the captain and part owner had come to Alaska from Binghamton, New York. He had fished with me for several years on the Pelagos. After a sudden end of employment with Arctic Alaska Fisheries, I was looking for a similar position (rotating captain) that would allow time off for family. Don liked the idea and hired me on the spot.

At 180-feet, the Evening Star carried a crew of twenty-six. It was one of many vessels built for one purpose and later converted to use as a fishing boat. A large number of vessels came, like the Evening Star, from the offshore oil industry. Others were former military vessels, surplus from World War II or the Coast Guard. I had spent a season fishing golden king crab on the Northern Enterprise, another converted offshore oil supply vessel, and so I had some experience with them. They are designed with a flat bottom and shallow draft for their size, so they tend to slide through a turn and drift quickly in the wind. But they are stable and carry a lot of pots. Don called his boat the Big Blue Bus.

The marine architect developing stability and loading criteria for the boat, said he would rate the vessel to carry five-hundred pots. "But," he added, "Between you and me, I don't care if you stack pots to the clouds, you won't turn this boat over." That was comforting. What was not comforting was sighting an unusual spot of scaly rust on the port bow just above the water line. Commandeering a painting float, I paddled out to the bow for a closer look. Inserting my finger into the spot, I poked a hole completely through the steel, starting a stream of water flowing from the hole. Fortunately, it was a small spot, and it was quickly repaired. A thorough inspection of the surrounding area revealed no additional rot.

The main deck of the Evening Star was completely enclosed. Fishing operations were conducted from the upper deck, sixteen feet above the water. While the decks of many crab boats are constantly awash, the deck of the Evening Star was high and dry. The factory was spacious and well planned. In addition to the brine freezers common to all catcher-processors, the Evening Star also had an air blast freezer and was the only catcher-processor so equipped. Four small live tanks enabled it to continue to process crab long after fishing stopped. Its biggest deficiency was the small size of the refrigerated cargo hold. The hold was in the stern of the main deck. It had a smaller capacity than freezers in comparable catcher-processors and required more frequent offloads that cut into fishing time.

Oil Spill

Preparing for the voyage north, we loaded fuel at Time Oil in Lake Union, Seattle. It was a bright, sunny Sunday afternoon. As we loaded over a hundred thousand gallons of diesel fuel, a misidentified valve was accidentally opened. A stream of fuel from a four-inch diameter pipe shot from the side of the boat and spread a multicolored sheen upon the placid waters of the lake. The quick response of the crew was impressive. One of the men leapt into the water. Pulling an oil boom with his teeth, he swam around the boat capturing the oil inside the floating containment.

The entire crew was mobilized. Equipped with floatation vests, boots, gloves, and hard hats, and armed with absorbent pads; they commenced mopping up the oily mess. By the time the Coast Guard was on the scene, the situation was well controlled. The Coast Guard incident investigator surveyed the operation from the shore. He saw the spill contained, and the two-dozen workers carefully cleaning. Then he strode down the dock, ignoring piles of trash bags filled with oil soaked pads and the busy workers collecting the colorful contaminant from the lake's surface. "I thought you said you had an oil spill here?" he asked abruptly.

"Yes," I said, interested to know where the question was leading, "we certainly had a spill."

He stepped closer toward me and with a stone-serious expression said, "I don't see anything here." He walked off the dock, climbed into his truck and drove away. The officer's recognition of our efforts to recover from a severe ecological accident was gratifying. We completed the clean up and finished fueling. Final preparations for processing were completed as we crossed the broad expanse of the North Pacific Ocean. Five hundred new pots were stacked on the deck, rigged and ready for capturing crab.

Fishing in a Boneyard

Bairdi are similar in appearance to snow crab but typically larger. They have red eyes instead of green and a differently shaped mouth. Crabs with characteristics of both (hybrids) are found in some areas. They might have one red eye and one green eye. Or they might have brown eyes. Other distinctive characteristics become confused in hybrids as well, but experienced fishermen usually recognize the differences. Along with their larger size, bairdi are prized for their sweet, succulent flavor. The size and appearance of king crab are awesome, but the majority of crab fishermen prefer the distinctive flavor of bairdi.

Bairdi are accomplished climbers and active escape artists. Anyone can catch a king crab if they set a pot in the right place, but that is not true of bairdi. King crab like going into pots, even pots without bait. If the crew neglects baiting a king crab pot, and crab are in the area, the pot will still have half as much as a baited pot. I have found old pots with barnacle-encrusted buoys and tattered web from which any crab could easily escape, but strong healthy king crab were still inside—just hanging out. Bairdi, on the other hand, are more temperamental and don't appreciate containment. They can be enticed into a pot by bait, but they will soon start looking for an exit.

After the king crab season, the Evening Star fished bairdi. We moved around with the fleet until locating a lonely spot to the northeast that proved highly productive Ocean north, so that he would come over and take a look. At 210-feet, the Royal Enterprise was the largest Bering Sea crab boat. The Royal Enterprise was a former Arctic Alaska catcher-processor now operating under Tyson Seafoods, who had recently acquired Arctic Alaska's assets. I was disheartened when they steamed by setting pots through our gear. Soon, I thought, the whole Tyson fleet would charge in and decimate our secluded little school.

The following day we crossed paths with the Royal Enterprise again, as he piled his pots back on the boat. I could see that the pots they hauled were empty. I kept hauling pots as well, but as each pot surfaced, I spun the boat to block the captain's view of its contents. I could not let him see our bulging pots of bairdi as they were lifted onto our launcher. My radio crackled. "Jake," he asked, "What are you doing in this boneyard?"

"Oh," I replied, "there were a few crab around. I'm not sure how much longer I will stay."

The Royal Enterprise picked up all their gear and vanished over the horizon. Of course, I neglected to tell him that had he left his gear soaking for another twelve hours, he would not have referred to the area as a boneyard. The crabs were being temperamental, as bairdi can be. At least three tide cycles were needed to persuade the reluctant crustaceans to climb in. A pot pulled any sooner than that was empty. My friends from Tyson hauled one tide too early. Fishing continued to be excellent for the next month. We fished through Christmas and produced more pounds than any other boat that season. Following bairdi, we launched directly into the opilio (snow crab) season.

Christmas Dinner

Christmas Eve marked the third day of fifty to sixty-knot winds. The stress of operating a vessel under hazardous conditions, combined with depressing thoughts of spending Christmas away from my wife and children took a toll on my health. High winds and thick snow squalls persisted on Christmas day. The dark arctic night and foul weather kept my attention focused on fishing, and I was almost grateful for the dismal distraction of work.

By late morning I was still hauling gear, ill with chills and fever and fatigued from a long night's work. All morning the cook battled dinner in a rolling, pitching galley, and she was now close to completion. Savory smells of Christmas swirled through the upper decks and into the wheelhouse, but all I desired was a healing sleep. The deck was secured, and a watch posted. I fell into my bunk. I was barely asleep when a timid knock sounded on my door. "Sir," said Big Mike, the foreman, quietly, "The men are asking that you pray over dinner." How thoughtless I had been. I selfishly retired to my room, wallowing in self-pity. There were others who hurt, others who missed family, and others who had needs I had neglected. I assumed that this meal would be like any other. I was wrong.

As I descended the ladder to a crowded galley, the mood was one of humility and reverence. A beckoning Christmas feast was set before the men, as savory scents filled the air, but all eyes were on me. Hope and expectation filled their faces. These were good men, but most spent little time in church. Several had scrapes with the law and were eschewed by society. But here and now, for these few Christmas minutes, they recognized a debt of gratitude. For a few minutes, with heads bowed and their rough hands quietly folded, they were children. And as I prayed, I knew God loved these humble sons.

Visions of Jesus

On catcher-boats with a crew of only five or six, taking a new person, especially a greenhorn, is an uncomfortable risk. But hiring greenhorns on boats with processing crews was common, and churning through quitters to form a stable crew could be challenging. The head office often sent workers with no prior experience at sea. Felipe was one of these. Felipe was in the wheelhouse as the Evening Star rounded the red buoy and headed out of Unalaska Bay. The weather could not have been better. There was barely a breath of wind or a wrinkle in the green glassy surface of the sea. Perhaps it was the vibration of the boat or the sight of the shore that seemed to be moving as the boat passed by the beach. Perhaps he ate some bad bologna. Whatever it was, poor Felipe darted for the door and doused the deck with his dinner. "You will get over it," we assured him. But he didn't. For the entire trip, Felipe remained in his bunk, bucket by his side. After a week of being seasick and unwilling to eat, he reported visions of Jesus coming to take him home. We didn't want Jesus to have him quite yet, so we dropped poor Felipe off on St. Paul Island. No one can blame a person for being seasick. It is one of those things that happen. Most adults get over it after a while, but it is a miserable condition that afflicted much of my childhood, and I have nothing by sympathy for anyone suffering from motion sickness.

Working in the factory of a fishing boat is not fun. It is noisy, cramped, wet, and always moving. The hours are long, and the pay is unpredictable. Many processors are content with doing the same thing hour after hour, day after day, and month after month. Others aspire to be deckhands. Those who seem capable are given time on deck and perhaps a boost in pay. When an opening is available on deck, a processor often fills it. Some eventually become captains or seafood company executives. It's a good place to start.

Big Mike's Big Headache

Big Mike was the processing foreman. Large and powerful but polite and gentle, he came to Alaskan fishing from the shipyards of Louisiana where he worked as a welder. Using a winch running on an overhead track, it was his job to move the baskets of crab through the various stages of cooking, cooling and freezing. Like fishing in foul weather, storms also increase the difficulty and danger of processing. During one storm, the boat pitched to starboard, causing Mike to lose control of a 350-pound steel cage of frozen crab. It ran down the overhead rail, smashing against the blast freezer. The boat then lurched to port, propelling the basket back toward Mike, who had stumbled on a step. The steel bar of the cage caught him in the head, leaving a long gash across the top of his skull. A galaxy of bright stars filled his field of vision before the celestial scene suddenly went black and the big man succumbed to unconsciousness.

Big Mike regained consciousness as the crew helped him into the galley. Blood streamed over his face and down his back. Ice packs and pressure, along with Lidocaine and epinephrine injections, eventually stemmed the bleeding enough to allow me to suture the long laceration. Years before, I received a brief ad hoc training in suturing from a plastic surgeon. Although the years of fishing presented previous situations requiring the skill, I had never sewn a wound of this size and never worked on a scalp.

I boiled a disposable razor and wiped the area with an iodine solution. Then, between the pitches and rolls of the boat, I removed the surrounding hair with the razor, cleaned the wound, and stitched the severed skin together. Big Mike sat patiently through the procedure. I sent him to bed with forty new sutures, a head wrapped in bandages, antibiotics, and pain medication. Healing was progressing nicely until Mike stepped out of the shower and hit his head on the steel shower curtain rod. This, he said, was more painful than the original injury. Many of the sutures had to be redone. Despite his accident, Mike stayed on the boat and after a suitable period of rest and recovery, he returned to running the factory.

Mario's Flight

The cities and villages of the Aleutian Islands frequently experience buffeting by high winds that might be named hurricanes and garner headline news in more populous and less remote areas. When winds in Dutch Harbor exceed one hundred knots, causing sheets of plywood become airborne, and the airport terminal roof to be peeled away again, it's not a news flash, it's just Wednesday.

The Evening Star lay tied to a small dock at the head of Dutch Harbor. Northwest winds screamed across the beach in front of us, picking up pallet boards and plastic totes from the tops of storage containers. The Icicle processing barge Arctic Star was sideways to the wind off our starboard bow. It broke loose from its moorings and was being held against the dock by two struggling tugs. A man in a truck drove alongside the boat, rolled down his window and started yelling something. We were tearing the dock apart, he said. He wanted us to move. That was not going to happen.

Occasionally one of our three-inch thick mooring lines snapped, and the deckhands were summoned to replace it. After working on a broken line, the deck crew was headed back inside. But before he could make it, Mario was plucked from the back deck by a sudden powerful gust of wind. He flew over the five-foot-high bulwark surrounding the deck and was dropped into the water a hundred feet from the boat. A surfer and a strong swimmer even in his clothes, Mario was able to swim to the other side of the harbor and fight his way back to the boat without being struck by flying debris.

Losing Pots and Gaining a Son

It was a bad year for sea ice. We were fishing in an area that should have been safe from ice, but strong northerly winds bringing sub-zero arctic air quickly pushed the pack ice south, and floes suddenly surrounded our buoys. Searching up leads and between floes, we scrambled to gather our gear before it was swallowed under the solidly frozen sea that was rapidly approaching. A few of our northerly strings had to be abandoned to save others. By the next day the wind abated and the pack ice slowed to a crawl. The carnage caught most of us by surprise, with some boats losing hundreds of pots under the frozen white wall. We recovered most of our gear, but dozens of our pots were buried beneath the solid sheet of ice.

For the next several weeks, we pulled empty pots from barren seabed while waiting for the ice to ebb. It was during this wait that I received a telex from my wife. It read, "Your anniversary surprise arrived last night. It takes after you anatomically. Please advise what to call it." We had a son! Families of fishermen have to be flexible. Holidays can be postponed, birthdays celebrated early, and events planned for the off-season. But babies come, with or without dad. I was able to attend the arrival of our five previous progeny, and I was scheduled to fly home in plenty of time for this one, but the calculation of his due date was a month off.

To Russia

After the 1992 snow crab season and a brief break, Icicle Seafoods decided to send the Evening Star to the Russian Far East. With the Diomedes, another

American crab catcher-processor, and two Russian crab boats, we were to col-laborate with a Russian research agency in conducting a sampling survey of a large area of the Sea of Okhotsk. After completion of the survey, we would be permitted to fish an allocation of blue king crab. It was not easy to take a job as mate—I like being in charge—on a five-month trip to Russia. But I was recovering from recession-era business problems, and struggling to regain a financial footing. I left my wife with six kids (including a new baby), legal problems, and an empty bank account. But she was capable and I had a job, and for those things I was grateful.

From Seattle, we traversed the North Pacific to Dutch Harbor, where we loaded pots and topped off the fuel tanks. Leaving Dutch Harbor, we fol-lowed the great circle route north of the Aleutian chain, past the Komandorski Islands, and down the west coast of Kamchatka to the island village of Severo-Kurilsk. We were not allowed to go ashore. We anchored until joined by four Russian fisheries scientists and a government representative.

The Chess Master

The survey portion of the trip involved setting strings of longline pot gear at sampling stations spread across the deeper areas of the eastern shelf of the Sea of Okhotsk. We caught few crab in most of the areas, but whelks (a snail) were everywhere, sometimes filling our crab pots. The distances between survey stations required tedious traveling time. Frequent chess bat-tles with the Russians and some of the other crewmembers were my favorite distraction.

Yuri, the Russian government representative, was a recognized chess master and the best player on the boat. At first, he showed little interest in the game. Then he covertly watched games I played with others. After a few weeks, he offered to play me. One of the Russians explained that players of his caliber were picky about who they played. He didn't consider me worthy. I imagine the boredom of boat life finally persuaded him to lower his standards. Yuri defeated me easily. But we continued to play, and I gradually picked up strategies and learned moves. One day, I won a game. By the end of the trip,

I was winning one of every three games. The concentration required by chess was a significant factor in maintaining my sanity that summer.

Boarded

On a clear, calm day a large warship, bristling with armament, appeared on the horizon, heading toward us. Our interpreter advised that we prepare to be boarded. Soon a small boat came alongside while the intimidating cruiser followed close to starboard. A dozen uniformed soldiers, armed with automatic weapons and great furry hats, quickly formed a crisp line on our deck. Six officers followed, making their way to the wheelhouse. When the officers were off the deck, the soldiers relaxed and started serious trade negotiations with the crew. The iconic Russian hats were a hot item, as were their large coats. But they refused to part with their Kalashnikovs.

In the wheelhouse, using broken English, one of the officers requested copies of our contract to fish in Russia. I presented the fifty-page document, and he began copying it by hand on a notepad. "Would you like to use our copy machine?" I suggested.

"You have copy machine?" he questioned, astonished by the possibility. "There are only seven in Moscow!" Fascinated, he followed each paper as it emerged from the machine. His delight was such that I wondered if the coveted copier would be confiscated. But he collected the copies, patted the machine admiringly and let it stay. After decorating our documents with official looking rubber stamps, hot sealing wax, and pretty ribbons, the boarding party returned to their ship and sailed away.

Bribery

While we fished for crab, Yuri, the Russian government overseer, fished for bribes. "This area is closed," he informed us through our interpreter. "But for $500, I will let you fish here." We picked up the gear and moved. "For $500, you may keep codfish for bait." "For $500, I will overlook your keeping of small crab." It was always $500.

Approaching the tanker Arma for fuel, the captain demanded $500 as a tax to tie alongside before fueling could begin. We threw the lines and pulled away. Don and I wanted nothing to do with bribery. We carried no large sums of cash on the boat, so if payment of bribes occurred, it was done by someone else, perhaps the Russian company we contracted with. After a few hours, we were invited alongside the Arma and fueled the boat without further problem. Yuri eventually realized the futility of his requests and gave up.

A Matter of Interpretation

Our Russian shipmates spoke little English, so we relied on an American interpreter for communication. An impish young man, our interpreter had complete control over the dialog. The Russians were demanding, hostile, and dissatisfied with conditions on the boat. The translator worked tirelessly to solve problems and negotiate through difficult situations.

We were confused by how quickly simple issues escalated into serious confrontations. It seemed that the Russians were impervious to reason. We were frustrated at having to navigate constantly through misunderstanding and suspicion. Partway through the trip, the interpreter had to return to the States and was replaced by another. Now the difficulties dissolved and we discovered the friendly cooperation each side actually desired from the start. We concluded that the first interpreter was trying to be more than a mere facilitator of conversation. He wanted to be a diplomat and perceived as a hero. The conflict was his construction and creating a solution was his satisfaction.

Confusing Quotas

The agreement with the Russian scientific agency sponsoring our charter stipulated that the four vessels in our group had exclusive rights to fish crab in four designated districts of the Sea of Okhotsk. So we were surprised when a group of American crab catcher-processors came sailing over the horizon and started setting pots in our private part of the sea. The captain, Don, called the intruders on the radio. "What are you guys doing here," he inquired.

"I guess we could ask the same thing," came the reply, "we have exclusive rights to fish in this area."

"What?" responded Don, "We have exclusive rights to fish here!"

A few weeks later, another group of American boats appeared. Apparently, we all purchased exclusive rights to fish the same quota in the same area. We reported the situation to our company. A few days later their reply appeared on our telex. "These other deals" it read, "were done in the back streets of Moscow. There is nothing we can do about it."

Frozen

Offloading product required workers to spend most of the day in the frigid freezer. Every hour they took a fifteen-minute break in the warm galley to defrost and don dry gloves. It was late in the evening when the offload was complete, and we cast off from the freighter. At the encouragement of his companions, one of the processors came to the wheelhouse, complaining that his fingers were numb and immovable. I was shocked. His fingers were frozen solid. During the frequent breaks, he neglected to change into dry gloves, and the dampness of the wet cotton drew the heat from his hands. How he moved boxes of crab without bending his fingers was a mystery to me. How could he go so long without recognition of a problem?

Following the first-aid book's procedure for frostbite, his hands were soaked in warm water and dried. He was a heavy smoker with poor circulation in his extremities, and I feared the worst. After warming, I sent him to bed with instructions to call me if any blistering appeared. Within a few hours, blisters covered his fingers. We began the process of moving him to a medical facility.

There was a hospital in Severo-Kurilsk, less than a mile away, but the diplomatic distance was a bigger problem than the ten-minute boat ride. American mariners were not allowed on shore. High levels of influence were needed to bridge the rigid bureaucracy. After several hours of waiting for official action, a skiff of well-armed police approached the boat and picked up the injured man. Soon he was admitted to the Severo-Kurilsk hospital. Our request that the interpreter be allowed to accompany the patient was denied. Not only were we concerned about our friend's inability to communicate with medical personnel, but also we feared his race would result in sub-standard care. There are not many blacks in the Russian Far East and we were nervous about how he would be treated. But no more could be done.

We later received word that after two weeks in the hospital, doctors decided amputation was necessary, and they released the patient for travel to Seattle. All of his fingers on both hands were subsequently removed. About a year after the incident, I ran into the man while offloading salmon to an Icicle Seafoods processing ship. I was pleased to hear that the company treated him well, and that he was working again.

The Dentist

Over the years, I have dealt with dozens of serious at-sea medical issues from fractures to gynecological issues. Vessels operating far offshore carry well-stocked medical kits and are equipped for rendering first aid and treating common shipboard illnesses. Larger boats like factory trawlers may have trained medical personnel, but on smaller boats captains or engineers are usually the ones to administer treatment. Captains also have authority to prescribe medication. But authority does not impute ability. Usually, one tries to make an injured or sick person comfortable and get them off the boat as soon as possible. More recently, services became available for consultation with physicians on shore, but for most of my experience, I thumbed through a first-aid book and hoped I was doing the right thing.

When a Russian scientist developed a painful tooth, I gave him my best wishes for a speedy recovery along with a bottle of oxycodone and some clove oil. None of those remedies proved satisfactory. After the infected man repeatedly complained of persistent pain, I set up a small dental office on the port side of the wheelhouse and reluctantly opened for business. His mouth was disgusting. I expected better oral hygiene from a man of science. He asked me to extract the offending tooth, but it did not appear to be abscessed, and I thought it prudent to try filling it first. I cleaned and disinfected the cratered molar, and installed a temporary epoxy filling. The procedure eliminated his pain and the filling held at least throughout the remainder of our time in Russia.

Heading Home

The chilly winds of autumn were now blowing across the Sea of Okhotsk. Political winds were also blowing. The dissolution of the Soviet Union occurred in December of 1991. Now, rumors of coups and collapse fueled concern that reached even as far as the Sea of Okhotsk. The Russian scientists were troubled by the rumors, but hopeful for a future of positive change. Yuri, the government overseer, and a former member of the Communist Party, remained silent on the subject of politics.

We were concerned that political and military upheaval and possible conflict with the United States may leave us unable to return for some time. So I was especially excited when word finally came to pack up our pots and head for Dutch Harbor. Few things feel so satisfying as the arrival of the end of a season and finally heading home. But the end of this trip was especially welcome. I had only three minutes per month to speak with my wife over a new and very expensive satellite communications network. We both decided separately that this would be my last trip fishing in Russia.

At Severo-Kurilsk, a skiff came to collect our Russian friends. Despite a rocky start abetted by a troubled translator, and his continually clobbering me at chess, Yuri and I developed a warm friendship. As he grasped my hand to say goodbye, he held it, saying in English "Captain Jacobsen, you are a good man."

That trip was the longest five months of my fishing career and my last trip on the Evening Star. While still in Russia, I arranged to run a different boat. Subsequent to a similar survey the following year, the Evening Star was sold to a Russian company and continues to fish crab in Russian waters.

CHAPTER 14

THE PACIFIC SUN

I was offered a job running the Pacific Sun in 1991 for fishing crab in the Russian Sea of Okhotsk. I would start with the 1992 snow crab season. The Pacific Sun was a ninety-eight foot Bering Sea crab boat. I was fully aware that boats like the Pacific Sun were small, unstable, and poorly built. Several were resting quietly at the bottom of the Bering Sea along with the sailors that went down with them. Despite the poor reputation and potential risk, I decided to take the job. The possibility of making more money and being closer to home outweighed the comfort and safety of a larger vessel.

When I first saw the Pacific Sun a few months later, my heart sank. It was dry-docked in a Dutch Harbor, Alaska shipyard. Because of an error by the previous captain, the propeller and shaft were bent and being repaired. The main engine was severely damaged as well, and would have to be rebuilt. The boat was filthy, rusting, and run down. Drug paraphernalia littered the galley. A stash of cocaine was found in a cabin. It was New Year's Day and the snow crab fishing season was scheduled to start January 15. Finding a competent crew was not easy fifteen days before a season. I was reticent to keep the old crew, but after interviews, I kept two, the engineer and Ricky, a deckhand.

The engine repair was proceeding slowly. Poor weather prevented needed parts from arriving in Dutch Harbor. With five days until the season opening, the mechanic announced that the engine was not repairable and would need to be replaced. Replacing the engine would take additional weeks we could not afford. After interjecting my opinion on the matter, the rebuild continued. I jealously watched the rest of the crab fleet steam out of town as I stood helplessly on a broken boat.

...Dutch Harbor a long torturous week after the ... The previous captain left two loads of crab pots on the king crab grounds with few clues as to their location. Fortunately, the weather was clear, cold and calm, and after a day of running to the grounds and another day of hunting, a stack of pots was on the deck. Most of the fleet was fishing over 300-miles away, but with the second load of pots still left to find, I was impatient and unwilling to go that far.

As soon as I thought I could find a snow crab, I set the gear. There was not another boat in sight, or on the radar. They were all far to the northwest. Another two days was needed to locate the remainder of the gear, and after filling the deck again, I headed back to where we dropped the first load. The pots we set previously were full of large, clean crab! We set our load nearby and began hauling up beautiful pots of snow crab. In just four days the boat was full, and we headed to the small village of Akutan (a day's travel away) to offload. Akutan is thirty-five miles east of Dutch Harbor and home to a large Trident Seafoods crab and fish processing plant. The "Deep Sea," a crab processing ship owned by a much smaller company was anchored in Akutan Harbor. That was our market. Fishing continued to be strong and despite the occasional winter storm, we delivered several more trips to the Deep Sea. It was apparent that we were doing better than many other boats.

Generally, offloading is considered a time to rest, repair, resupply, and recover. The processing company provides offloaders, leaving deckhands free to do other things. But offloads can sometimes be more stressful than fishing. Such was the case delivering a load to the Deep Sea that year. In Akutan, I fired the engineer for endangering the vessel and crew. Despite his promise to stay clean, I caught him using drugs. He insisted that because he was a good friend of the owner, he was immune from firing. He swore he would have me fired instead. When the firing was finished, I was on the boat and he was headed home. I took over the engineer's duties.

Later, while the processor pulled brailers (a collapsible basket holding around 1,500 pounds of crab) of crab off the boat, the wind picked up to sixty-knots with gusts to one hundred knots (115 miles per hour). It was rough even in the protected waters of the bay. During the offload, we kept the main engine running and I maintained a careful watch in the wheelhouse. We continually crashed against the Deep Sea's giant rubber Yokohama fenders and tested the hold of their anchor. Several of our two-inch diameter mooring lines snapped, so it was necessary to keep the boat ready to maneuver in the event the ship's anchor lost its hold or we were torn suddenly from the processors side. During a violent gust, instead of breaking, one of our lines tore its mooring cleat off the Deep Sea's deck. The steel cleat shot across our deck, striking Tom, one of my deckhands, on the back of his shoulder. The force of the impact knocked him out and fractured his scapula. Had it hit his head, he may have been killed.

Tendering

The end of the snow crab season was a welcome relief. We took the boat to Seward, Alaska where another captain and crew used it for longlining halibut and black cod. I got the boat back a month later for the summer salmon tendering season and then king crab. Tendering gave us the opportunity to make some needed repairs. I found a new engineer, Tony, who was very competent and a machinist by trade. He was just what the boat needed.

Tendering is generally enjoyable, but offers some unique challenges as well. One of the deckhands came to the wheelhouse to complain of bleeding from a cut on his anus. He wanted me to tend to his wound. I had no desire to look at his anus. I was curious how he would explain a wound in that particular location. He claimed that he had eaten a corn chip that failed to digest. It traveled, he asserted, through the entirety of his gastrointestinal system without losing any of its rigidity. Passing through the anus, it inflicted a painful incision. The story was creative but entirely implausible. I have rendered shipboard first-aid for cases from frostbite to fractures. I filled cavities in repugnant mouths, gave injections, and stitched skin across skulls. But I draw the line at anuses. I sent him home to seek care for his crack from a medical professional.

Looking Over My Shoulder

As the resource recovered from the collapse of the king crab fishery in the early 1980s and new participants poured in, the fishery steadily ramped up in intensity and shortened in length. The 1992 season was expected to last less than a week, leaving no room for mechanical problems or errors in fishing strategy. Since so much hinged on the success of this fishery, Dennis, the owner of the Pacific Sun, decided to ride along for the season. Having a well-rested watchman would allow the rest of us to sleep longer, but having the boss looking over my shoulder caused some trepidation.

A friend of Dennis's captained another boat that fished crab that year. His boat was equipped with an underwater camera. Towing the camera behind the boat allowed him to see schools of crab as they crawled along the seabed. Prior to the fishery, this boat scanned the fishing ground in search of the optimal place to start the season. Because of his long relationship with Dennis, he shared the coordinates he considered the best place to fish.

The day before our departure, Dennis approached me in the wheelhouse. He marked some positions on the chart. "This is where Greg saw massive schools of king crab," he said. "Now where are you going to fish?" I indicated a spot far to the north. Dennis appeared perplexed. He checked the report from the previous summer's king crab survey, an annual report that includes charts of the fishing grounds, divided into survey areas. It indicates how many crab were found in each area. The survey indicated that zero crab was found in the spot I proposed. The area was empty. The areas around it showed zero crab too, as did the areas around them. Based on the survey data and the camera sightings, there could not be a worse place to fish than the one I indicated. "I guess you know what you are doing," Dennis said. I wondered if that comment was a statement or a question. "I have been doing this for a long time," I replied with hopeful hubris.

Of course, I had no idea if crab would be there or not, but I felt it was a good place to look. Besides, only beginners fished on survey crab. Survey data indicates where crab was found the summer before, but crabs have legs and they can move quickly over the grounds. Finding crab is critical, but a large part of success in crab fishing is figuring out where they are going and keeping ahead of them. On the other hand, there was the camera information, only days old. Cameras enjoyed a brief popularity years before, but their sightings failed to correlate with increased catch and most boats removed them. I was not impressed with the second-hand camera clue and ignored it.

We had eighty un-baited pots stored in a designated pot storage area north of the grounds, and a similar amount on the stern of the Pacific Sun. I planned to set the deck load off at the spot I showed Dennis, and then shuffle down two loads from the pot storage and spread them around until I found a school. We charged out of Dutch Harbor into sloppy seas. Thirty hours from Dutch Harbor, I roused the crew and we set out the first load of pots. Then we were off to the pot storage area. In eight hours we were back to where we dropped our first load and checked a pot. In a short season especially, the first pot up is the most eagerly anticipated. It can set the mood for the trip. Our first pot was empty.

We left the disappointing pot in the launcher, ran a few miles and set out the entire load in short prospecting strings. Then we ran to get our remaining pots from storage. Returning again to our baited gear, the pots we checked were all empty. I ran a few miles to the southwest and set out the rest. At the end of day two, we had less than a dozen crab on board. On day three we shuffled pots around some more, but found only a few hundred crab.

Dennis was visibly troubled, but not nearly as much as I was. So far the season was a disaster. I should have set on the survey crab, or the camera crab, I thought. At least then I would have an excuse. But instead I set in a barren wasteland. I was a failure as a fisherman. My resume detailing decades in the fishery was about to be dismantled in a few disastrous days on the Pacific Sun. Dennis said nothing, but finding a replacement for me must have occupied much of his thought. Still, I was committed to the area, and there was no time for a major move.

We worked day and night with little rest; pulling empty pots and shuffling them short distances. The demoralized crew slowed work to a grumbling crawl. The season would be over in a few days and at this rate we would have little to show for it, probably not clearing expenses. In the evening of day three, we hauled the gear set the previous day. A few crab appeared on the bottom of the first pot. The next pot had a few more. Then pots started coming up plugged with big beautiful king crab. We stopped hauling and ran back for more gear, saturating the area until all our pots were on crab. Suddenly the crew was energized!

We hauled full pots of crab all of day four, working non-stop. On day five it was over. We almost filled the boat, and may have, but during the night as we worked a few miles away, another boat ran through our last sixty pots, stealing the crab and leaving the pot doors open. When the final tally was taken, the Pacific Sun was well above average, and more than doubled the catch of the camera boat. And, despite putting Dennis through the drama of a nearly disastrous season, I was not fired.

Water in the Wheelhouse

In February of 1993, toward the middle of the snow crab season, we headed to offload in the face of a frightening forecast. Strong northerly winds were coming that would cover the boat in ice and push the rapidly descending icepack over our gear. The Pacific Sun was not quite full, but with two tanks flooded and an ice load, it would be too dangerous to move pots. I wanted to get offloaded and return to the grounds before the weather hit. I didn't make it. Mechanical issues delayed our scheduled offload to the Deep Sea by twelve hours.

On the 28th of February, with the wind blowing sixty-knots and temperatures down to twenty-degrees below zero, we bumped out of Akutan Bay into an active storm system. I would not usually consider charging out into such severe weather, especially in a smaller boat like the Pacific Sun, but radio reports indicated that the sea ice was moving rapidly southward. Friends I was fishing with warned that ice was just twenty miles from my gear and moving at one mile per hour. With high winds from the north, ice floes pack together to form a wall of ice that can quickly cover the fishing grounds. Crab pots left in its path are unlikely to be seen again. My season would be over. I was compelled to push through the weather and get to my gear. Even running slowly into the sea we frequently took green water over the wheelhouse. Thick ice formed on our sides, but heavy seas knocked it off again.

Suddenly an enormous wave reared up slightly off the starboard side, right in my face. It was a killer, probably fifty feet tall, and pointing right at me. It rose so rapidly I didn't have time to move out of the way. All I could do was cover my head and duck. The wave hit the wheelhouse with a deafening crash. Icy seawater enveloped me. Shocked and shivering, I was surprised at the realization that I was unharmed. As the water drained from the bow, I was puzzled to see all the windows intact. I was sopping wet, and water sloshed across the wheelhouse floor. Where did it come from? It was surreal.

All of our windows except one were made of one-half-inch thick tempered glass. The odd window was directly in front of me. It was made of one-half-inch thick Lexan Plexiglas. I figured that the force of the wave bowed the plastic inward allowing about thirty gallons of water to flood in around its frame. Had it popped out, I may not have survived to write about it.

Everything appeared to be okay except for the steering. The rudder swung hard to port and stayed there. I took the engine out of gear. When I attempted to switch the autopilot off, dull quick pulses of electricity shot through my arm and rattled my body until the circuit breaker tripped. Working with electricity while standing in a pool of salt water and wearing salt-water soaked clothes was not a good idea. The boat pitched wildly as I tried to determine the cause of the problem. The Pacific Sun did not have a manual hydraulic helm like many boats. The only steering system was electric. Ice accumulated quickly on our windward side as we floundered in the freezing seas. Within a few hours, we would be in grave danger of capsizing.

I traced the problem to a steering function selection switch. It interfaced the gyrocompass, steering compass, jog levers, and autopilot. Smoke wafted from its cover. As we worked to restore steering, I kept the engineer running from the wheelhouse to the engine room and back. "Go turn the pump off. Go turn it on. Now turn it off again." Each order included a trip to the engine room. At one point things became confused. A misunderstanding about whether the pump was off or on resulted in my receiving another severe electric shock. Recoiling from the jolt, I inadvertently threw an aerosol can of electrical contact cleaner so hard it hit the wall and ruptured, filling the wheelhouse with pungent chemicals.

The selector switch was about three inches in diameter and eight inches long. Four long screws passed through multiple rings, and each ring had several colored wires coming out of it. I disassembled the unit, but it appeared damaged beyond repair. Metal parts were melted. Plastic pieces were fused together. It was a mess. I tried to reassemble the switch, but the rings were not lining up properly and I was unable to get a nut on one of the long screws. Despite the misalignment, I wired it back in. The engineer ran below and turned on the power. I moved the jog lever and nothing happened. It didn't work. Almost out of hope, I activated the autopilot. The rudder angle indicator swung to center. Miraculously, the autopilot worked!

When hauling gear, a jog stick (or jog lever) is used. It gives more precise steering control and a quicker rudder response time. But I was happy to at least have some kind of steering. It increased our chances of survival considerably and negated the need for a rescue. As far as fishing was concerned, I would make it work.

The wind diminished by morning and we made full-speed for our pots. The ice stopped just short of our most northerly string, and we worked non-stop shuffling them to safety. The crew was able to sleep during runs, but in six days after leaving Akutan, I slept only seven hours. Our next delivery was scheduled in Dutch Harbor, as there were no facilities for electrical repair in Akutan. One of the generators was also having issues, and I arranged for a mechanic to take a look. With the boat tied to a dock, a technician tested the steering. It no longer worked in autopilot mode or any other mode. I was told there was no way it could have worked at all. "Then how did I get here?" I asked. Fortunately, a replacement was available and within a few hours complete functionality was restored.

We finished the season without any further disasters and returned with almost all of our pots. The 1994 Bristol Bay king crab season was closed and

I decided to stay home for a while. I thanked Dennis for the opportunity and moved on. The Pacific Sun later received much needed reconstruction, including the replacement of everything aft of the house from the keel to the crane (the boat was cut in half and aft end was replaced with a new aft end). It was also widened, creating a much more stable platform. The new and improved boat continues to fish crab in the Bering Sea.

CHAPTER 15

THE FISH HAWK

An important element of navigation—one to which navigation charts frequently defer—is called by navigators local knowledge. I met the crew of the ocean-going tugboat Fish Hawk on a pebbled beach in Dutch Harbor, Alaska. "Are you a captain?" they asked intently. My response "Yes, I'm the guy you're looking for" brought visible relief to their faces. After being at anchor for three weeks, the tugboat crew could finally leave Dutch Harbor and continue their journey pulling a huge barge across the Bering Sea and up the Yukon River. The barge was loaded with desperately needed fuel and supplies for several villages and for the salmon fishery on which their local economies and traditional way of life depended.

The previous captain experienced serious medical issues while the tug was crossing the North Pacific. A new captain was needed to complete the voyage. At the time, few fishermen were also licensed Masters, and most of those were restricted to uninspected fishing industry vessels. I had an inspected license, meaning I could operate other types of vessels, including tugs, in addition to fishing boats. I was finished relieving my brother as captain on a 285-foot factory trawler, and had been asked by an anxious tugboat owner to fill in.

The final instructions of Mr. Bodey, the tugboat's owner, were to make sure the barge does not touch any ice. A previous captain, he said, caused extensive damage to the barge towing it through ice fields. There would be no tolerance for any damage from ice. And there was plenty of ice. The ice edge extended well south of Nunivak Island, leaving two hundred miles of ice between our barge and its destination. The ice break-up was late that year, not only did cover the outside waters, but it still clogged the mouth of the Yukon

River, where I was to meet a pilot boat to guide me through the shifting sands and changing channels of the challenging river.

The Yukon River salmon fishermen were concerned about the delay in Dutch Harbor. Without the fuel and supplies on my barge, they would not be able to prosecute the fishery that was the lifeblood of their community. If the salmon arrived at the river before I did, great hardship would ensue. I pulled the barge out of Unalaska Bay, already feeling the tension between my mandate to keep the barge away from ice and the fishermen's anxiety over receiving supplies in a timely manner. After travelling two days toward Nunivak Island, we anchored behind Cape Newenham, waiting for the ice to clear. The Emmonak fish camp called twice daily to check on my progress (or lack of it) and to reiterate concerns over missing the salmon run. I was increasingly torn between the admonitions of the owner to avoid ice, and the appeals of fishermen to push through it. Finally, after four days at anchor, with the owner's orders still fresh in my mind, but persuaded by the impassioned pleas of my fellow fishermen, I hauled the anchor and headed north.

The light spring breezes of the previous week allowed the ice to loosen up and spread. I followed the edge until I found a lead large enough to travel through. But the lead soon ended. Running out additional tow cable, I used the tug to push the icebergs, some the size of houses, to the side, creating a channel. Cautiously I maneuvered the barge through. Yes, the barge touched ice. It touched a lot of ice. But I went slowly and was careful to avoid damage.

After a day and a night of pushing ice and running through meandering leads, we approached Cape Romanzof. I pushed toward the beach and found clear water along the shore. With only a fathom or two below the barge, it was still necessary to proceed slowly. We reached the mouth of the Yukon in the evening of our second day in the ice. In the previous few days, most of the ice was pushed out of the great river's mouth, making passage possible. But I wasn't going in tonight. Using the tow cable as an anchor, we waited until the morning and a high tide. The shallow-draft pilot boat appeared through the morning fog just after dawn. A sand bar stretches across the wide expanse of the river's opening. The tug could get over, he said, but the barge was too deep. We would have to pull it across the sand.

Pulling a barge filled with 265,000 gallons of gasoline and carrying thirty shipping containers, a few dozen boats, some heavy equipment, and a crane across a sand bar was a new and confusing concept to me. What, I wondered with silent sarcasm, could possibly go wrong there? The pilot was the son of the barge's owner. He had been piloting in the river for many years, so I had to trust that he knew what he was doing. Sure enough, the barge grounded exactly where he said it would. He threw us a line that we tied to our bow bollard. With the pilot boat pulling the tug, the tug pulling the barge, and both of us at full throttle, the barge reluctantly slid across the soft sand of the bar.

The Emmonak fish camp was forty miles upriver. The Yukon bore little resemblance to the Columbia, the only other large river in my inland navigation experience. Narrow channels in a broad river, submerged sandbars, deep cuts so close to shore that tree branches scraped the barge, and variable currents were all feature of an invisible obstacle course and kept me nervous. The pilot zigzagged ahead of me and gave careful instructions.

A crowd of cheering people lined the riverbank as we approached the fish camp. I had never received such a welcome. A collective sigh of relief ascended as the barge was secured to its moorings, but no one was more relieved than me. The barge was undamaged, and a competitor's barge was far behind. Mr. Bodey expressed his gratitude and kindly offered me a permanent position with attractive pay. I appreciated the offer, but refused. Running a tugboat was interesting, but I am a fisherman and fishermen need to fish.

CHAPTER 16

THE JENNIFER A

A Rough Start

After leaving the Pacific Sun, I spent some time at home. But soon the pressure of mounting bills had me looking for another boat to run. The Gold 'N Star was similar to the Pacific Sun. It was built by the same shipyard, using the same design, but was one year older (built in 1978). I immediately liked the boat's new owner, Pat Dwyer. He had worked for most of his life in various aspects of the fishing industry and, as I came to learn, was very knowledgeable, especially of things in the engine room. He also had a personal and passionate concern for crew safety stemming from the disastrous loss of his previous vessel the St. George. The St. George disappeared with its crew of six in January of 1992. An empty life raft and a satellite locator beacon were all that remained.

The Bristol Bay king crab season was cancelled for the second straight year, so we set our sights on snow crab. Sailing out of Seattle, the newly named Jennifer A had many improvements, but was still a small, older boat in a big ocean. Crossing the North Pacific to Dutch Harbor with a full load of pots went well. We tended to a few details and waited for tank check. (Tank check is an inspection, prerequisite to all crab seasons, during which an Alaska Department of Fish and Game representative visits the boat, checks for all required documents and licenses, and verifies that the crab tanks are empty).

We were an hour out of Dutch Harbor when the main engine low coolant level alarm sounded. The engineer filled the engine's expansion tank, but soon it was empty again. The leak was not in the engine room, and the engine oil was free of water. The likely location of the leak was the void spaces below the forward crab tank. While the rest of the fleet continued to the fishing grounds, we turned around and headed back to town for repairs. It took two days to find and repair the leaks; a disappointing beginning to what would be a long and challenging season.

Most of our snow crab that year was delivered to the Arctic Star, an Icicle Seafoods processing barge tied to a dock in St. Paul Harbor. For what seemed like most of the season, the harbor was frozen. A tugboat, the Fidalgo, served as our icebreaker, plowing a path to the processor. During one cold trip our deck crane's slewing motors (that rotate the boom) froze. It slowed us down, but we kept working. After our next delivery, we spent two days in St. Paul trying to unfreeze it. By the time we were done, ice, several feet deep, surrounded us on all sides and fastened us firmly to the Arctic Star. The Jennifer A's 850-horsepower was insufficient to pull away. The Fidalgo worked over an hour to pry us loose. Finally, we broke free and followed the tug out of the harbor.

Kiki's Courage

The deck of a Bering Sea crab boat is a harsh judge of stamina, courage, and character. Novice deckhands, if they successfully complete an entire season, don't usually return. And few of those who do will ever excel. On the dock, it's difficult for a captain to tell who can cut it. On the deck, it is easy.

Kiki was a small, sinewy Samoan. He was quiet and likeable, with a large quick smile and an easy-going attitude. He had several years of crab fishing experience on other boats before joining my crew on the Jennifer A. At 102-feet, the Jennifer A was one of the smaller crab boats in the Bering Sea fleet. It was very active, rolling and pitching wildly in heavy seas. The movement was too much for Kiki, whose previous experience was on bigger boats. At the beginning of each season, he was seasick for several days. After one particularly rough two-day trip to the fishing grounds in fifty-knot winds, the crew went to work on deck, setting off a load of ninety crab pots. Kiki had not eaten during the entire trip, and after several hours of hard physical work, he became dizzy, and then blind. Finally, Kiki collapsed unconscious on the deck.

Resting in the galley, he regained consciousness, but still could not see. After eating a can of fruit cocktail and other sugary foods, his sight gradually returned. At my request, he retired to his bunk, but a few minutes later he was back on deck and working hard.

The Jennifer A's design left little tolerance for ice build-up. Cold weather mandated caution in stacking pots and careful attention to the overall ice load. On a bitterly cold February morning, we were fishing one-hundred miles northwest of St. Paul Island. The wind was from the north at thirty-five knots. Thick polar ice was rapidly advancing toward our gear, and I was trying to move it to a more southerly location before it became covered and lost. Sea ice changes in character depending on the speed, duration, and direction of the wind. Sometimes the ice is spread out and relatively gentle. Miles before one reaches the ice pack, scattered areas of ice cubes appear, followed by floes of pancakes that grow larger and closer together as the solid edge approaches. Leads between the floes can be easily transited and when necessary, boats bump through the floes to get to their gear. The buoys that mark the location of each pot are not typically moved or cut off by lazy, spread-out ice floes. But when northerly winds howl with frigid ferocity, the pack ice pushes south, compacting the cubes, pancakes, and floes into a white wall of destruction that kills buoys and cuts lines.

My crew that season was Peter, the engineer, Jerry, the deck boss, Kiki, and my cousin Mike. On a cold February afternoon, the crew finished chopping off the latest layers of ice that during the day had accumulated to over a foot in thickness. After a brief break, they were again hauling gear. The hydraulic hauler quickly retrieved the sixty-six fathoms of line, and a pot broke the surface of the sea. A boom extending from the ship's mast carries a winch that lifted the pot from the sea. The catch looked average—around 350 crabs. Today I was more concerned with moving the gear than counting crab. We were stacking the pots on deck to move them south to a safer place. When stacking gear, each pot is cleaned of crab and the bait jar is removed. The line is tied up in a coil, and the line and buoys are tossed into the pot for storage until setting. We typically hauled twelve to fifteen pots per hour, but today things were slower. There were only three men on deck instead of the usual four. The previous day Kiki slipped on the icy deck, and an 800-pound crab pot fell on top of him, crushing his pelvis and legs. I could find nothing broken, but he was badly bruised and unable to use one leg. I gave him pain medication and consigned him to his bunk.

As Peter, the chief engineer, bent over to pick up a coil of line, a large chunk of ice broke away from the boom—a part they couldn't reach when clearing the ice few hours before. The massive block landed on his lower back. Peter's limp body washed across the deck. Was he dead? I raced to the deck fearing the worst. Fortunately, he was only unconscious. We placed a stabilizing board beneath his back and carried him into the galley. Peter was now in and out of consciousness, vomiting, and urinating blood. We carefully removed his wet clothing and warmed him with blankets.

The boat subscribed to a consultation service with a physician standing by at all times to respond to marine medical emergencies. I relayed the details of Peter's accident, his vital signs, and current condition. Following the doctor's instructions, I checked for broken bones and internal bleeding. Other than some possible spinal injuries, Peter's bones were intact, and there was no indication of internal bleeding. There was severe trauma to the kidneys and back, but the doctor did not consider the injuries to be life threatening.

St. Paul Island was twelve hours away. It had an airport and medical clinic, but was now surrounded by thick ice that even the powerful tug could not penetrate. The harbor was impassable, and all aircraft were grounded. I would have to head to Dutch Harbor, thirty hours away. But I had a problem. The ice pack was closing in. In twelve hours, the sixty pots remaining in this northern area would be lost. Replacing them would cost tens of thousands of dollars—deducted from the wages of the crew and myself. The physician determined that a delay would not adversely affect Peter's prognosis. But I had another problem. At least three deckhands were needed to haul and stack the pots. I had only two left and they were short on sleep. One was a greenhorn.

I explained the situation to Kiki. He understood the cost of abandoning the gear. I'm sure he thought of his family and all of us dependent on the season's pay. He painfully pulled himself from the bunk and prepared for work. That night, Kiki displayed courage that few possess. Compelled by Peter's injuries and impending ice, I drove the crew nonstop through the night. The seas were sloppy but very workable. The air temperature dipped to minus twenty degrees Fahrenheit. Kiki did not complain. He did not quit, despite frequent falls. Working with constant piercing pain, he persisted through the night, hopping and limping up and down the rolling deck, his tears freezing as they rolled from his cheeks. There were neither cheering crowds nor gold medals in the offing. There was no patriotic duty or life in the balance. There was simply a young man with a hero's heart, who was willing to sacrifice comfort and endure pain for his family and friends—and a proud captain who loved him for it.

Shallow Crab

Some fishermen seem to be gifted with an extraordinary ability to catch crab or fish. I was not. If I were paid for effort instead of results, I would be a wealthy man. But judged by results, I was fairly average. I had some shining moments and other seasons I would rather not discuss. My standard of success was to work as hard as I could and bring the boat back to the dock with all hands. In that respect, I was always successful.

The ingredients of a perfect season are flat, calm waters, warm weather, no mechanical problems, no crew problems, and catching more crab than anyone else. The closest approximation to a perfect season for me was the 1995 Pribilof Islands red and blue king crab season. With the Bristol Bay red king crab season closed that year, the Pribilof Island season would contribute the bulk of the boat's income for the remainder of the year. The weeklong fishery started September 15. I first set gear between St. Paul and St. George Islands, but it was scratchy and I couldn't find a school of crab. I stacked the gear on deck and set out in search of a better spot. My partner boats were seeing some encouraging signs northeast of St. Paul Island, so I ran around Northeast Point and set a few strings.

The next day I returned and hauled the gear. The crab count looked promising, and the numbers were leading me shallower. I was now with a group of around twenty boats, including my fishing partners, who were working outside the large bight between St. Paul Island's North Point and Northeast Point. It was congested in the crowd, and my better pots were shallower, so I moved closer to the beach. There was a surprising number of crab in the shallows, and I positioned the rest of our pots between the beach and the other boats.

Rolling through the gear daily, we kept on top of the shallow school. Were other boats doing better further off shore? Should I move pots into the fracas and fight for real estate with the rest of the crowd? I thought we were doing at least as well. As it turned out, we were faring better. After anchoring in Lukanin Bay (on the south side of St. Paul) for a day, we delivered to the Icicle processing barge Arctic Star. The crabs were large, averaging seven to eight pounds each, and we caught more than any of us estimated, and more than any other boat that season.

Two deckhands on the boat had never fished crab. One had experience in the Bristol Bay salmon fishery. The other was a life-long fisherman from the east coast, who owned a tuna boat and fished along the eastern seaboard. Intrigued by stories from the Bering Sea crab fishery, they were both anxious to try it. This season was not the ideal example—it was far too easy. Beautiful weather, relaxed work, good food, plenty of sleep, and a fat paycheck seemed the ultimate enticement for further participation. But they both quit. It was, they complained, too hard. Too hard! I was incredulous. Crab fishing didn't come any easier.

The Crew Quits

I maintained a policy of zero tolerance for impairment due to drugs or alcohol. The only impairment permitted under my policy was sleep deprivation. My crews were allowed to drink a beer at the bar, but anyone returning to the boat inebriated was terminated immediately.

The policy was tested one evening during a snow crab season when Timo returned to the boat drunk, shortly before our scheduled departure for fishing. I gave him thirty minutes to gather his gear and get off the boat. He was Samoan, as were the engineer and the rest of the deckhands at the time. In a show of solidarity with their intoxicated countryman, they gathered in the wheelhouse. "If Timo is fired, we all quit," proclaimed Jerry, the deck boss.

"Fine," I replied, "you all have thirty minutes to pack your junk and get off my boat."

Twenty-five minutes passed before I heard Jerry climbing the stairs to the wheelhouse. "Skipper," he said, "I am really sorry. We don't want to quit. We want to stay on the boat."

"Fine," I said. "Take Timo off the boat and find someone sober to replace him." They did.

Arrested

There is a legal size limit for all commercial crab species fished in Alaska. Sublegal crab is to be returned to the sea unharmed. Fishermen should be very careful to measure questionable crab and discard those that are too small, but mistakes are made. Small crabs will grab the leg of a larger crab and be tossed into the tank along with it. These are called Klingons (or Cling-ons). Large waves can sweep over the sorting table, and wash small crab into the tank. Tired deckhands sometimes become confused and throw legal crab overboard and illegal crab into the tank. I have seen tired deckhands toss an undersized crab in the tank and the measuring stick overboard, and most of us have thrown a measuring stick in the tank a time or two. Some crews tie the measuring stick to a string attached to the sorting table or to their belts.

When the crab is delivered, the offloaders throw dead and small crab aside into a corner of the tank for later removal. Fisheries biologists check deliveries and sample the crab. Perceived violations are reported to the National Marine Fisheries Service (NMFS) Enforcement Division.

When the Jennifer A delivered a load of bairdi to a processor in Dutch Harbor, a deckhand witnessed the biologist sampling from the pile of small crab accumulating in the corner of the tank. Consequently, the biologist reported a much higher incidence of small crab than if the sampling was done anywhere else in the tank. No mention of small crab was made during the offload. The report was not released until some time after the crab was cooked and frozen, so the results could not be subsequently confirmed or disputed with additional data.

The captain has nothing to do with measuring crab. The captain is responsible, however, for fisheries violations, including an excessive percentage of small crab. Hearing rumors, I checked with the enforcement office in Dutch Harbor and spoke with the officer, a man I had known for many years. "Hi Jake," he said, grinning. "I just issued a warrant for your arrest on felony charges."

"Well, that's happy news," I replied sarcastically. We chatted about the charges. I was headed to the Pribilof Islands to try fishing for deep-water golden king crab, but promised to call in for my trial.

The day of the trial, I took the boat into St. Paul Harbor and found an operating telephone at the fuel dock. Representing myself over the telephone in a felony trial was probably not the smartest way to proceed. I plead no contest. I asked the judge to consider the fact that in decades of crab fishing I had no previous violations, and that there was no reasonable expectation I would have been aware of small crab intentionally being retained. I also raised the sampling issue. The prosecution agreed that the felony charge was inappropriate, but was statutorily mandated based on the reportedly high percentage of illegal crab.

Despite a stressful hearing over a static-ridden payphone, charges were reduced to an infraction, on par with a parking ticket. But I was fined $5,000. The incident made me ill.

After two years of Bristol Bay king crab closures and a poor bairdi season, my arrest for a fisheries violation was the final blow. I was burned-out and needed a break. At the invitation of a friend, I decided to try something else.

CHAPTER 17

THE PACIFIC LADY

The Northern Lady Sinks

Scott was a fishing partner. Boats often partner together to share fishing information. On February 13, during the 1995 opilio season, his boat, the Northern Lady, caught fire and sank northwest of St. Paul Island. Scott and his five crewmembers were able to get off the boat and were rescued.

Scott and a partner subsequently purchased the Pacific Wind (a 130-foot crab catcher-processor) and renamed it the Pacific Lady. The Pacific Lady started its commercial life as a crab-harvesting vessel named Skipbladner. In 1985, it was purchased by Arctic Alaska Fisheries and configured as a crab catcher-processor. A few years later it was lengthened thirty feet by cutting the vessel in half and inserting a midsection. Under Scott's ownership, the boat retained its ability to catch and process crab but added the capacity to catch fish with longline gear.

Flying Hammers

There were some interesting people on the Pacific Lady. There were former gang members, some who had served time in prison on various charges, and several with a criminal past. One proudly displayed a number of circular scars from bullet wounds received in a drive-by shooting. But only Lonnie made me nervous. He spent time in prison for manslaughter and clearly had difficulty managing anger. The incident that precipitated his dismissal came soon after he joined the crew. When deckhands carelessly allowed undersize crab in the hopper, the processors tapped their crab measures on the steel bulkhead of the factory to let them know they should sort better. The frequent tapping increasingly irritated Lonnie until he boiled over in a fit of irrational rage. Brandishing an eight-pound sledgehammer and screaming obscenities, he began beating on the factory bulkhead. The other deckhands ran for cover as Lonnie released his frustration through the heavy hammer. Without considering the stupidity of confronting a crazed sledgehammer-slinging convicted killer, I flew from the wheelhouse to the deck.

Without touching Lonnie, but inches from his face and with frightening ferocity, I described the inappropriate nature of his actions and suggested he take a time-out—or something to that effect. Lonnie set the hammer on the deck and apologized. He was well behaved for the rest of the trip. When we arrived in Dutch Harbor for offloading, Lonnie disappeared and never returned. I had not yet formally fired him, but I'm sure he figured it was coming and saved me the trouble. I had his gear boxed up and left on the dock. Over a decade later, I passed Lonnie on a Seattle sidewalk and stopped to chat. He seemed happy to renew acquaintances, and we enjoyed a pleasant conversation without the mention of sledgehammers or belongings left on a dock. I was happy to hear that he was employed and doing well, and delighted to see his cheerful smile.

A Look at Longlining

After the crab season, I took the boat to Seattle where aluminum modules for longline fishing were installed on the deck. In the early 1990's the Bering Sea longline fisheries were developing rapidly and Scott wanted in on the action. With the conversion complete, we headed north to fish for cod and turbot. Longlining with hooks is similar to longlining with pots. A groundline carries evenly spaced short lines, each holding a hook (instead of a crab pot). And because hooks are smaller than crab pots, many more populate the groundline. Small longline operations may use a tub system where the groundline is coiled in a wash bucket, and hooks are placed around the top rim of the tub.

The hooks are baited by hand and set off the stern. Larger operations typically use an automated system that holds hooks in magazines. The hooks are baited automatically as they are set out the stern. Strings of longline gear are set with anchors and buoys at each end. An average Bering Sea factory-longliner might set and haul forty to fifty miles of longline gear daily. After the gear has had sufficient time to fish, the buoys at one end of the string are hauled aboard and the anchor is retrieved. The line is placed in a hydraulic power block that pulls it from the seabed. The groundline is guided over a shiny steel roller, and one by one, fish file onto the boat. From the roller, the line runs through a crucifier and hook cleaner. Despite its ominous title, the crucifier does not pin the poor fish's fins to a fish cross. It separates the hook from the fish's mouth by pulling it through an opening too small for the fish to fit through. Freed from the hook, the fish fall into a hopper and are carried by conveyor into the factory where they are processed into frozen blocks, minus the heads and guts. The hooks are automatically guided back onto a magazine, ready to be set again. The Pacific Lady used 35,000 hooks that were set and hauled daily.

Longlining codfish can be boring for captains, at least is was for me. Once the line is in the block, it is usually a simple matter of driving the boat at the right speed in the right direction and watching the line for tangles or other problems. As long as the gear was on fish, life was good, though somewhat mechanical. We didn't stop fishing, even in eighty-knot winds.

Attacked by Killers

Fishing turbot proved more challenging than fishing cod. There was an organized and intelligent adversary determined to dine on the delicacy our line dragged from the deep. Turbot and black cod are typically fished further down the shelf than gray (Pacific) cod. So perhaps it is the distance that makes these fish more desirable to the orca, whose primary diet in the Bering Sea is salmon. Things harder to obtain are often imputed otherwise inexplicable value. Or maybe they just prefer the flavor.

For whatever reason, pods of killer whales that ignore the hundreds of thousands of codfish pulled from the bottom each day by longliners, become fully mobilized the minute a turbot is attached to a hook. They sometimes move in silence, submerged and unseen. Other times they approach overtly, bounding forward like a terrible armada that defies defense.

The result is the same: a line with hooks full of fine turbot is suddenly hauling in only heads.

When we see them coming, or recognize a stealth attack, we quickly buoy off the end of the groundline and let it go. We drift, whistle, and act innocent. But they sense the turbot and seem to know what we are up to. They circle the boat several times and start the stakeout. We run to another string. They follow. We shut down and drift, hoping they will become disinterested and wander off. They don't. We try to haul a string, but the sound of our hydraulics acts like a dinner bell. We haul what we can, but too soon it is only heads. Another boat is fishing in the distance. We buoy off the groundline and run for an hour to try to pass our posse off on them. We hurry back to the first string, but a sentry is waiting at the buoy, its black and white head bobbing in the water. Is that a grin?

The whales don't negotiate. They want all the fish, except for the bad ones. Some turbot have ragged fins, blotchy coloration, and look sickly and old. The whales let us keep these, but we can tell the turbot have been tasted. Scrapes from sharp teeth run down the skin of the fish on both sides, but there are no bites. Orca lack a sense of smell, but they are picky eaters and apparently have discriminating palates. Over the weeks, I get to know my pod and give them names: Scarback, Gimpy Fin, Doc, Grumpy, Two-Spot, Happy, Dopey. The federal fisheries observer objects to some of the more disparaging monikers. The killers are, after all, protected marine mammals. I don't care. I hate them.

I try a different strategy—satiation. We haul gear as fast as we can and let the whales feed, hoping to salvage a few fish. How much can they hold? Turbot are large fish, weighing twenty to thirty pounds. The whales must get full at some point. But they seem to understand my tactic and put out the word. Other pods arrive. As the entire Bering Sea orca population heads to my position, I figure out that feeding the whales does not work. More experienced turbot fishermen concur. It was a stupid idea. The orca are more organized than I thought.

Trawling for pollock, I loved the giant killer dolphins. Sea lions are the bane of the trawl fleet. When the cod end pops to the surface, sea lions use their teeth to rip through the heavy double mesh, creating holes that spew fish like a hydrant. But their fun is over when the whales arrive. They hug the cod end tightly, trying to disappear into it as the whales draw near. The whales don't play with turbot. A snap of the powerful jaws and the fish is gone. But they play with sea lions. I have seen an orca throw a large screaming bull into the air, catch him with a crunch, and throw him again. It is a bloody, brutal spectacle. If killer whales had limbs and humans tasted like turbot, mankind may never have made it past Cro-Magnon. The whale wars went on for months, but somehow we scraped together a season and made it home with a few dollars in our pockets.

Longline Crew

At the time the Pacific Lady was fishing, longlining was one of the lower paying fisheries for both the deckhands and the processing crew. New processors attracted by fables of fishing up fortunes on a crab boat, apparently assumed the opportunities of all Bering Sea boats were the same. They were quickly disillusioned when they found themselves in the factory of a longliner. Some quit after a trip or two when struck by the realization that processing codfish was long, tedious, miserable, and the money mediocre. Fortunately for longliners, conditions and pay have improved, but like all Bering Sea fisheries, it is still no picnic. For many, the distance from everything familiar is too much to bear. A sense of adventure, desperation for money, and tolerance for unpleasant circumstances are all requirements for work on any at-sea processing vessel.

After the turbot fishery, I left the Pacific Lady to pursue a career in marine surveying, and to manage logistics for the boat. Unfortunately, the new captain was unable to produce sufficient revenue to pay bills, and problems compounded quickly. Despite our ordeal with the orca, our turbot season made money, but it was the last profitable season for the Pacific Lady. Crews quit, vendors cut off credit, and within two years of my departure, U.S. Marshalls seized the vessel. My brother and I, along with one deckhand, were contracted to bring the boat from Dutch Harbor to Seattle, where it remained until being sold at auction. The vessel continues to fish today under the name Blue Attu, named for Attu, the last island in the Aleutian chain.

CHAPTER 18

STEPPING INTO MARINE SURVEYING

Becoming a surveyor

The profession of marine surveying is at least hundreds of years old and probably more. In the age of sailing ships, insurance companies concerned about fraudulent claims sent inspectors to ascertain that the insured vessel existed and to place a value on the cargo it carried. This practice expanded to include inspections relating to other aspects of the marine trade including vessel safety, accident investigation, construction and repair, regulatory compliance, vessel valuation, suitability for service evaluations, expert witness work, and more.

As the Jennifer A neared completion of its shipyard projects, a credentialed marine surveyor was hired to perform an inspection and appraisal for insurance purposes. He spent about thirty minutes interviewing me in the wheelhouse. I told him about the extensive work that had been done and what was left to do before departure. After the interview, the surveyor climbed down the wheelhouse ladder, and looked around the galley. I followed after to see if his inspection spawned any additional questions. He opened the door to the engine room and looked down. He did not go into the engine room; he merely looked down the ladder. Then he walked off the boat and never returned.

A report was issued a few days later. It was full of mistakes, misrepresentations, and descriptions of equipment the surveyor never saw. I thought about that experience quite a bit that year. Friends of mine were dying on boats. If I could do a better inspection, I might be able to prevent some deaths or injuries. In 1995, I formed a marine survey company of one, Fishermen's Maritime Services, Inc. Studying books and other materials on marine surveying, I hoped it would eventually replace fishing as my primary source of income.

I discovered later that my experience with the sub-standard surveyor was an exception. Marine surveyors are typically dedicated and competent professionals who excel at their craft. My first opportunity was to survey the Pacific Lady. Crawling through the boat stem to stern, I issued a detailed and descriptive report. At the time, I was inordinately proud of this first effort. Today I am embarrassed by the report that bears my name. Thankfully, my surveying skills improved, along with my reports. During my periods in shore, I surveyed a few more vessels. When the Pacific Lady suffered catastrophic damage to a main engine, a very kind surveyor was assigned to the insurance claim. After relating my aspirations in the field, he encouraged me to jump into it full time. Several months later, I did.

My decision to leave fishing was cemented one evening while turbot fishing on the Pacific Lady. Just after being relieved by the mate and retiring to my stateroom, my heart started beating wildly, with irregular pounding. I felt faint, and fell into my bunk. I considered alerting the mate, but decided against it. We were far out to sea in stormy weather. If my condition were fatal, I doubted a medevac would change things. If it were not, I would feel foolish. I really hate to feel foolish, especially in front of the crew. I fell asleep wondering if I would wake up again. I survived the night, but was too weak to walk. I could only crawl up to the wheelhouse the next morning, and had to be helped into my chair. Perhaps, I thought, I should get a job a little closer to a hospital.

A few insurance company executives noticed my work and recommended me to clients needing surveys. With their kind assistance and generous recommendations, I was able to make it work. Over the years, survey assignments have taken me to ships in Europe and South America, and on boats ranging from an eight-foot inflatable raft used by law enforcement to a 680-foot fish processing ship. In addition to fishing vessels of all types and sizes, barges, tug boats, cruise ships (to 719-feet in length), pleasure craft, multi-million dollar yachts, dredges, research vessels, floating docks, law enforcement vessels, ferries, transports, passenger boats, and floating cranes have all come under my scrutiny. I have been involved in numerous legal cases, accident and fire investigations, and even inspected fire-damaged fishing nets in a muddy Oregon landfill. It has been a fascinating journey!

CHAPTER 19

THE VALIANT

Rice and Beans

The 1998 St. Matthew Island blue king crab season was the end of my many years at sea. The boat's owner and regular captain wanted some time off for hunting and let me take his boat for the short season. The Valiant was a schooner (house aft) style boat with a comfortable ride. It was one of ten eighty-six-foot steel crab vessels built to a Ben Jensen design at Seattle's Pacific Fishermen's Coop shipyard in cooperation with Flohr Metal Fabrication. A twenty-foot long section was inserted in the mid-body in 1994. The aft house was replaced with a full-width deckhouse, and a new wheelhouse was installed on top. Despite its additional length, the boat was easy to handle and fun to drive around.

The Valiant had an all Mexican crew, most who had been on the boat for several years. They were good men who worked hard, but after a week, I grew weary of rice and beans for breakfast, lunch, and dinner. All the deckhands were experienced except for Candido, who had never been crab fishing before. On the day of departure, Candido arrived at the boat in a sporty late-model muscle car, from which he and an entourage emerged. Candido was wearing new clothes more suitable for a disco party than a fishing boat. A very attractive young lady clung tighter to him than the gold chain draped around his neck. I thought he was a drug dealer turned state's evidence in a horribly misguided placement by the witness protection program. Would this guy even make it past Dutch Harbor? I silently wondered.

Once fishing started, some of the crew complained about Candido. He was, after all, a greenhorn, and experienced crewmen often complain about their untrained companions. From the wheelhouse, it looked like he was learning. He didn't hesitate to do the dirty work relegated to beginners and kept a good attitude in the face of criticism. It was clear that Candido had class. Because of poor fishing, the season was closed in just eleven days, leaving some of the quota un-caught. The St. Matthew area can be like that. We were fortunate to find a few crabs. The weather was pleasant, and despite the abundance of beans, it was an enjoyable end to a long career at sea. A few years later I inquired about Candido. He was still on the boat and doing well. I was pleased.

CHAPTER 20

FISH TENDERS

Where Do Crab Boats Go in the Summer?

During summer months when crab seasons are closed, many crab boats go tendering. Typically tenders are used for the Alaskan herring and salmon fisheries. Some tendering of codfish may also occur during other times of the year, but usually not by Bering Sea crab boats. Boats that fish herring and salmon are comparatively small and are constrained in size by regulation. Most seiners are fifty-eight feet long. Gillnetters are usually thirty to forty feet long. Gillnetters working the waters of Bristol Bay are limited to thirty-two feet in length, but the width is not regulated, a fact that spawns some unusually plump boats.

The size of the vessel limits holding capacity. To maximize productivity during the season, harvesting vessels offload to tenders who wait at or close to where the fishing occurs. Tenders hold the fish in refrigerated seawater and transport them to a processing facility that may be more than a day's journey away, or right next-door. Tenders operate all along the coast of Alaska, but the busiest place is at the head of Bristol Bay. Tenders crowd the rivers of Bristol Bay, waiting for the gillnetters to finish fishing. After fishing, gillnetters tie to the tender's stern in what may become a long line of boats eager to offload. Tenders also supply fuel, water, and groceries to the gillnetters. Some offer laundry services and showers, facilities not found on many of the smaller boats.

Herring Tendering

Over the years, I've tendered herring around Ketchikan, Togiak, and as far north as Norton Sound. Seiners caught most of the herring delivered to me, but I also took fish from gillnetters. A fishery also harvests herring roe after it is deposited on kelp, but I was never involved in it. When herring are abundant, a seiner may not take its catch on board. Many sets are too massive to fit in the boat, corralling over a thousand tons of the flashy fish.

The seine is a large net with corks on the top and weights on the bottom. Spotter planes overhead direct the boats to the darker colored concentrations of the herring school. A skiff pulls the seine off the boat and into a large circle, hopefully around some fish, and brings it back to the boat. After the circle is complete, the boat dries up the net, closing the bottom and pulling much of it back onto the boat. The net is called a purse seine due to its purse-like closure that captures the catch.

When the shiny fish are concentrated, and the net closed, the tender pulls alongside the net and ties the net along its side railing. To keep the fish confused and to prevent organized escape, the boat crew, the skiff man, and even the tender boat's crew, can employ long aluminum plungers, repeatedly repelling the fish from the sides of the net. The tender lowers a hydraulic fish pump into the net that vacuums up the unsuspecting herring and sends them through a large (eight to ten inch) diameter hose and into the tender's tanks.

Sometimes seiners set their net right next to the beach. It can be nerve-wracking for a tender captain to put his bow on the beach in order to get alongside a net. He must watch carefully, so a receding tide does not leave him stranded. Loading 400,000 pounds of herring on the boat can cause it to get stuck on the bottom as well. Competent tender captains understand their limitations, know the area, and track the tides. Still, the aggressive and over-confident nature of many crab boat captains get them stuck. I have had to call friends to pull me off a beach, and I have helped others.

Herring seasons open when the fish come in from the sea to shallower water, and the roe is judged to be ripe. Most of the value of the fishery is from the roe, which is exported to the Orient, primarily Japan. Weeks can pass waiting for a season to start. When it does, it can be fast and furious. Seiners and skiffs bump and push for position, spotter planes circle overhead like buzzards, and tenders maneuver around nets and boats. It is all very exciting, and suddenly it stops. A season might include any number of openings, each of which may last only a few hours or a few days.

After the season, it's time for an extensive cleaning. Herring roe comes with a coating of superglue that cures on contact with a tender. Extruded by excited fish, eggs get everywhere and adhere to everything. Herring eggs wear off the deck, but the bulkheads, bulwarks, and tanks must be cleaned, and prior to pressure-washers it was a matter of scraping and scrubbing. Cleaning up after herring was my least favorite tendering chore.

Salmon Tendering in Bristol Bay

During the salmon season, the rivers of Bristol Bay come alive with activity. Gillnetters and tenders fill the navigable rivers. Floating processing ships and freighters congregate in an area designated the Y. Familiarity with the Egegik River made it my preferred station, although I spent plenty of time in the Ugashik and Naknek Rivers as well. Before GPS and electronic plotters, navigating the rivers involved a skeptical reading of the Loran, taking radar bearings, and keeping a watchful eye on the fathometer. Today's electronic equipment makes transiting the rivers less taxing as a navigation problem, although one must always be mindful of tides and traffic.

Anchoring in the river, a captain must take care to allow sufficiently deep water, and distance from other vessels, to accommodate the swing of the boat with changing tides. Many dedicated tenders and crab boats have flat bottoms, and can rest comfortably on the riverbed when the tide is low, but others may tip over if the water gets too shallow. Dragging anchor is a common occurrence. During strong tides, an anchor can lose its grip on the riverbed; suddenly sending it's boat drifting with the current. I avoided anchoring around boats with a reputation for inadequate anchor gear, because I disliked being disturbed. I have had to untangle my anchor from another boat's anchor after it dragged across and caught my anchor chain. It's an irritating problem to be confronted with just after getting to sleep. Often tendering is a relaxed and welcome break from the pressure and long hours of fishing. But tendering can be intense, especially in Bristol Bay. When fishing is hot, we take fish all day, run to the processor at night and return to the river in the morning. With all the activity, there may be little time left for sleep, at least for the captain.

Gillnetters use a simple net. It is a straight piece of web with floats on the top and weights at the bottom. Draped in a river's entrance, it ensnares salmon returning to the river to spawn. The fish try to swim through the meshes of the net, but find themselves stuck. Their body is too big to fit through the mesh and, if salmon even know how to back up, their gills prevent them from doing so. There are two types of gillnetter. Bow pickers have the net reel near the bow and the deckhouse aft. They set the net driving in reverse but pick it up again from the bow. Stern pickers, with the net reel aft and the house forward, are backward, or bow pickers are backward, depending on your perspective. After the boat drifts for a while with its net extended, the net is hauled back on a net reel and the fish are extracted. When the boat is full, or the opening is over, they chug up the river to their tender.

Salmon Tendering Other Places

Tendering took me to many beautiful parts of Alaska I may otherwise have never experienced during the summer months: Port Moller, False Pass, Chignik Lagoon, around Kodiak Island, and all over southeast Alaska. Lazy summer days anchored in a remote, stunningly beautiful bay offered opportunities for beachcombing, hiking, swimming, and other fun activities. There were periods spent attached to the cannery dock in Seward, Alaska, offloading fish and acting as a holding tank for the cannery. Other times we carried loads of fish to Prince Rupert or Vancouver, Canada for processing there. I enjoyed tendering's variety, scenery, and pace. The pay was less than fishing, but it was steady and dependable.

Swimming with the Fishes

Tenders hold salmon in refrigerated seawater, cooled to around thirty-one degrees Fahrenheit. At the processor, our seven-foot by seven-foot hatch cover was removed, revealing a chilly top layer of pink, scaly, froth typical of all salmon-filled tender tanks. The hold circulation pumps whip proteins from fish slime and blood into a delicate mauve meringue infused with glimmering salmon scales that sparkle if the sun happens to be shining. A fish pump hose is lowered into the tank, and the salmon fill the hose in a pulsating procession to the processor.

Thad, a new deckhand on the boat, was in charge of watching the hose. He tendered previously, but never fished. As we got to know him, it was evident that he was too slow, mentally and physically, to be a candidate for a crab job, but for tendering he was fine. He was the youngest of the crew and in good physical shape, so I gave him the task of moving the heavy fish-filled hose around the tank. If left in one place, the hose sucked up the surrounding salmon and then pumped only water. When Thad started teetering, I was on the top deck talking with some folks on the processor. At the edge of the tank, he lost his balance and was slowly falling backward into the four feet of foam covering thousands of frigid fish. Channeling his inner seagull, Thad frantically flapped his arms in a futile attempt to regain his balance. After several comedic seconds, gravity finally prevailed, and Thad joined the fish, creating a perfect man-shape through the dense salmon suds.

As Thad struggled to find the ladder through the freezing salmon and thick foam, the processor's all-female deck crew lined the rail for a sight of the shivering swimmer. Aided by a deckhand's direction, Thad located the ladder and climbed out. Back on deck, and unaware of his audience, Thad quickly shed his slime-covered clothes—all of them. The ladies cheered. Now, red-faced for two reasons, Thad scampered into the galley.

I liked Thad, so it saddened me to fire him a few weeks later. In consideration of the non-smoking crew, I did not allow smoking on the boat that summer. Thad, who claimed to be tobacco free, signed a contract stating he would not smoke. A few weeks after falling in the tank, I followed a familiar scent to the welding locker. Thad sat in the small locker between a cylinder containing 300 cubic feet of highly flammable, compressed acetylene and a similarly sized cylinder of oxygen. He held a brightly glowing cigarette. I forgave the contract violation and fired him for gross stupidity.

Cash Buying

It was 2:00 a.m. on a warm summers night. As I walked along the waterfront in a rough area of downtown Everett, WA, one hand clutched a pistol in my pocket. My other hand held a briefcase with $80,000 cash and signed blank checks to an account holding another $500,000. I was looking for a boat hired to take me tendering salmon in Puget Sound. After an hour of apprehensive searching, I found the boat and headed to the San Juan Islands.

Working the radio and waving fistfuls of cash at passing boats, I attracted the attention of enough fishermen to fill the small tender in two days. At the time, several fish buyers offered cash to attract deliveries. Salmon harvesters not committed to a particular cannery can sell their catch for cash on the spot, and carrying large amounts of money was common. Some buyers offered Hawaiian vacations or all-terrain vehicles as additional incentives for deliveries. New buyers especially used cash to overcome fishermen's concern about collecting payment. When cash buying salmon in Bristol Bay, I have had up to a million dollars on the boat. We had no safe, no security, and fortunately, no problems. Competition for fish sometimes led to bidding wars between buyers. But the fish buying business is driven by fluid market dynamics. In years of soft markets, cash buyers disappear, and fishermen struggle with profitability.

CHAPTER 21

GETTING ORGANIZED

The Rebirth of the AMA

The Alaska Marketing Association formed in 1972. I knew little about the organization in my early years of fishing. My father called it the Union, but it was not a union. The AMA negotiated crab prices with processors under an exemption from anti-trust law called the Fishermen's Collective Marketing Act. Sometimes they called upon the fleet to tie up, while they attempted to add a few pennies to the price after the season opened. I recall the frustration of sitting in Herendeen Bay tied to the crab processor Northern Shell for two months waiting for a strike to settle. When the AMA Board eventually agreed to send the fleet fishing, it was for a mere three cents per pound more than initially offered. I was angry at the paltry return for spending so much precious time away from my family. During the stand-down, I organized all the nuts, bolts, and washers in the engine room, memorized the few movies and television shows the processor had on VHS tape, and took an occasional hike around the bear infested beach.

In 1993, the organization had been inactive for several years, but low king crab prices spurred AMA President Gordon Blue to hold a re-organization meeting in December of that year. Six of us showed up: Gordon Blue, Gary Stewart, Scott Jacobsen, Sig Ingebretsen, Big Al Lauritzen and myself. At the meeting, Gary was elected president, and I was elected vice-president. Scott, Sig, and Al were appointed directors.

Perennially affable and composed, Gary Stewart was ideally suited to the position of president. Rallying the fleet around the prospect of a better price, a three-day strike prior to the 1994 snow crab season resulted in a few more cents per pound and a renewal of confidence in the fleet's prospects for the future of price negotiation. That spring, Gary and I discussed the organization's potential and trajectory. Those discussions resulted in my resignation as vice-president and subsequent appointment as executive director. None of us were familiar with crab markets, how prices were set, historical divisions of revenue, or even where to find market information, so I set about educating myself.

By the 1995 king crab season, the AMA had matured in knowledge, acquired market information and earned the acknowledgment of processors. Terry Schaff, president of Unisea Seafoods, was particularly receptive to working with us, but all of the processors were willing to talk. There were six major processors. As long as we could settle on a price with a major processor, the other processors would follow. Before the 1995 king crab season, Terry and I discussed the market situation. The yen was strengthening, and according to my calculations, the Japanese market appeared supportive of a price nearly twice that of the previous year. Terry asked what I thought the price should be. I made him a shocking offer, and offered a lengthy discourse on why it was justified. My unabashed asking for a record snow crab price proved to Terry that I was both fully in tune with the market and unafraid to hit the high note. He said, "I will call you back within three hours". He did call back, and he agreed to pay the price I sought. Within a day, the other processors agreed to pay the same price, and the fleet went fishing on schedule.

The process that year set a pattern for future negotiation. My analysis of the market was presented to the AMA board of directors. They authorized an asking price based on, and usually higher than, my recommendation. I approached processors and eventually we would come to an agreement. Some years a season opening date would come and go before a price was set. Strikes heightened tensions on both sides of the table. The fleet was itching to fish. Processors had idle crews, anxious markets, and accumulating expenses. Some fishermen failed to understand the value of the association's presence and persistence. Support from the fleet waned after periods of good prices and successful pre-season negotiations, causing membership to fluctuate between 50 and 250. Often a negotiation would begin with the processor posing the question "How many boats do you represent?" My typical answer was "All of them—but not all have paid their dues yet."

Some fishermen thought that we should never strike. Others believed a successful pre-season price negotiation indicated an inadequate price and that we should always strike. One naive fellow sent me a letter in which he expressed the opinion that we should simply ask the processors what they would like to pay and accept it without question. On rare occasions I received death threats—not from processors upset about some aspect of negotiation, but from fishermen eager to leave the dock. There were a few scabs, but for the most part the fleet was supportive.

Trident Seafoods, founded by Chuck Bundrant (along with Kaare Ness, my first crab skipper) represented the largest crab processing capacity. Chuck came from the crab fleet and built an Alaskan fishing empire with drive, innovation, and the strength of his dynamic personality. He was always accessible, friendly, and engaging with me, but my attorney had to wait outside—and the meat of the negotiation was typically with underlings. In any of my meetings with Chuck, the first matter of business was an inquiry about my father. My father helped Chuck through a few situations when he was just starting out as a fisherman, and Chuck never failed to express his gratitude. When fishermen and processors were at an impasse and pressure was mounting from an impatient fleet, I turned to Chuck for help, and he would oblige. But those were special circumstances, and most often he was content to let other processors take the lead.

Scott Jacobsen's experience as a former executive with Icicle Seafoods was invaluable during those early years. Gary, Sig, and Big Al remained in their respective positions until 2005 when the organization's necessity was supplanted by the crab rationalization program's arbitration system. The effort and effectiveness of the Alaska Marketing Association endures in the price formulas used in the rationalized crab fisheries of today.

CHAPTER 22

TRAWLING TIDBITS

Trawling in the Shallow End

Probably the oddest fishery I was involved in was trawling for yellowfin sole in the shallow waters adjacent to Round Island. Round Island is home to more than 4,000 walrus. I always enjoyed spotting the large pale grey animals in the cold waters of Bristol Bay. On the beach, they darken as blood flows to their skin. And the beaches of Round Island are packed with the unlikely animals.

A sole trawl has a heavy chain footrope that helps it tend bottom. It also has a head rope, dotted along its length with round plastic floats. The water in the area was so shallow that the floats on the head rope were visible behind the boat, each orange ball bobbing along on the surface. We tied a buoy to the end of our cod end so we could see how far back our net extended. With only a fathom or two under the keel, the shallow water was concerning, but it was interesting and helpful to watch the net as it followed us around.

The shallow seafloor in the area is surprisingly thick with sole, which didn't seem to be disturbed by the buzz of our engines or our large propellers cutting the water just above their flat little heads. At least they didn't swim out of our path. Eventually, regulators decided that the noise of fishing bothered the walrus, and the area was closed.

An Excerpt

I regret not keeping a consistent journal while fishing. There were just too many distractions and concerns to keep one updated. Most of my records

Jake Jacobsen

are in the form of letters to my wife. But I did attempt a journal a time or two. The following entries of a seven-day journal documented the final day of crossing the North Pacific en route to fishing, and the first few days of a 1988 pollock joint venture in the Bogoslof Island area.

February 14 - We are twenty miles from entering Unimak Pass. Although I lack a reliable clock, I believe the time to be approximately 8 pm. Night is dimming a foggy but pleasant day. The boats fishing here say the wind was a steady 75-knots with frequent gusts exceeding 100 knots. We had 35-knots on the stern which helped speed us along. All in all, it was an excellent crossing. I made contact with the Joint Venture and am to proceed to Bogoslof volcano where the mothership is anxious to receive fish. My thoughts frequently turn to my family although I try to distract myself with reading. Also, I won a game of chess with Brooks.

February 15 – Arrived at the fishing grounds but before we could set the net a hydraulic hose on the winch burst. Searching the boat for spare hose was fruitless. We went to Dutch Harbor, 50 miles away. A hose was made and waiting. Bumped the dock in Dutch to pick up the hose and headed back to fishing grounds. The net sounder is not working.

February 16 - Worked on the net sounder. Found faulty plug and blown fuse. I tried a tow without the sounder but caught nothing. The fleet is moving one hundred miles west. I haven't slept for two days and slept only two hours the night before that. Tired and frustrated. I need to catch fish but there are so many problems. While we were making the last set the main engine inexplicably died.

February 18 - Towed this morning but did not catch much. Changed doors. It helped. The next bag was full. The forward net reel broke but I fixed it. The lorans are messed up. I have to ask other boats where I am. The engine died while I had a full cod-end in the stern ramp. Still have a cough and flu. Threw up this morning. Slept four hours last night.

February 20 – Weather has been rough and cold. The boat is covered with one to two feet of ice. In order to make a delivery it is necessary to run out on the bow and break the ice off the windows 2 or 3 times during the delivery.

That was the final entry.

The Unwelcome Visitor

Improvements in net design have enabled boats to tow increasingly larger nets without boosting the horsepower needed. These new nets use long breast lines and large meshes. Rope trawl designs resulted from the realization that fish will funnel into a net opening, herded by vibration, even though they could easily swim through the mesh opening. Repairing these complex nets requires very careful sorting and bundling of lines and meshes. A crossed line will severely impede the net's ability to fish.

Bering Sea trawlers have a ramp cut into the stern that goes from the deck to the water. The ramp facilitates the setting and hauling of the net. Some trawlers use pumps to remove the fish from the cod end. Most just winch it up through the stern ramp, fifty to one hundred tons at a time. Sometimes other things come up the stern ramp.

It was 2:00 a.m. on a quiet, cool night in Kodiak Harbor. I finished three hours of tedious bundling and sorting in preparation for repairing a section of large meshes on the rope trawl. The net was spread strategically over the deck. The repair itself would take less than an hour, and I was anticipating a well-deserved rest.

As I measured a length of line, I felt as though I was being watched. Turning around, I was startled to see a bull sea lion twenty feet away and lumbering slowly in my direction. The six-foot-tall mountain of moving blubber, with large teeth and an attitude, somehow managed to climb up the stern ramp and onto the deck. He was about to cross the net that was carefully sorted and spread for mending.

Several mental pictures obscured my better judgment. Thoughts of the work I put into the net, the additional work required if a sea lion messed it up, and the problem of extracting a massive marine mammal from a rope trawl combined to create a spasm of insanity. Yelling and flapping my arms, I ran toward the one-ton animal. When I had closed to about six feet, the big bull hove to and sprinted out the stern. In retrospect, my decision to attack the beast was profoundly foolish, but it worked. I felt very large.

Sharks and Sea Lions

One spring I was running the Pelagos, trawling for pollock in Shelikof Straits, and delivering the fish to Kodiak. The Pelagos could hold half a million pounds of pollock, far more than the daily processing capacity of any one plant in Kodiak. So we made the rounds of every pollock processor in town, delivering 80,000 pounds to one plant, 120,000 pounds to another, until we were empty.

Sea lions frequented the boat during offloads, barking and begging for fish. I found a metal platform with a ladder and mounted it on the side of the boat so I could feed the sea lions like the trainers at Sea World. They leapt from the water and snatched the dangled fish from my hand.

During one offload, I found an eight-foot long salmon shark in the tank. Tying a line to its tail, I lifted it out with the crane and extended it over the water, thinking the sea lions would appreciate a great feast of shark meat. But as I lowered it toward the water, the sea lions scattered. They wanted nothing to do with a shark, not even a dead one. The shark was brought back aboard and three hours passed before the sea lions felt it safe to return.

Crossed Doors, Broken Wires, and Other Problems

Despite a dangerous reputation and long hours of hard work, crab fishing is relatively straightforward. Chaining off buoy lines and applying a sharp blade can sort out the worst tangles of pots. Longliners, endlessly hauling their dull gray groundline, deal with tangles and snags that occasionally interrupt the routine. But these are only irritations compared to the impressive problems sometimes encountered by trawlers. If a trawl is not set evenly, with both wires maintaining the same length, a one-ton trawl door on one wire may suddenly spiral over the wire on the other side, resulting in a calamity called crossed doors.

Before electronic length counters, markers were placed on the cables every twenty-five fathoms. Deckhands on each winch called out the length as they saw the mark. But sometimes marks wore off. Deckhands might miss a mark, get mixed up, or become distracted. Mechanical problems might also cause too much wire to run out on one side, or not enough. Crossed doors were not always the result of uneven wires, but when it was, it was a nightmare. Tangled steel cables, eight-foot tall doors, and a net must be hauled back and unwound. Sometimes it's a simple matter of lifting a door back to its proper side. Other times it comes back upside down or twisted incomprehensibly. In rough seas, straightening out the mess is incredibly dangerous. All of the deck machinery gets involved. Newer trawl systems with electronic winch controls and line counters alleviated many of the causes of crossed doors, but things still break, and problems still occur.

Before sonars warned of dangers ahead, it was not uncommon to snag a pinnacle, a wreck, or some other hard object, and snap a trawl wire. Hauling back on one wire is not as complicated a procedure as untangling crossed doors can be, but it still takes time and must be done carefully and correctly. I became an expert at spicing cable one season while trawling in a rocky area. Our trawl wires were rotten and broke dozens of times. We were fortunate that we never lost the whole net.

The most common problem in trawling is tearing up the net. A good rip provides hours of sewing for the crew. Most boats carry two or three nets so one can be fishing while another is being repaired. In some rocky areas, we could not sew fast enough. Finding competent net menders was a perennial problem. There were seasons when I was the only one with the skills to repair complex rips. The other crewmen filled my needles, held the web and fed me microwaved burritos. I learned net mending by holding web for my father and watching what he did. By high school, I was able to build nets, which my father sold. As I matured in my net mending skill, I started enjoying it. Mending in the winter with an icicle dangling from my nose was never enjoyable, but during warm and calm days I found it fun and therapeutic, like a puzzle combined with a craft.

Trawling Today

Towing a trawl through the dense traffic of boats hovering over the Bogoslof Island pollock school, I saw a large ship approaching. I made no effort to alter my course; confident it could easily move out of my way. The smaller boats were fishing and have the right of way. Big ships were processors. They were maneuverable and stayed out of the way of the harvesters. As the ship came closer, it was not giving way. I peered through the rain and haze of the darkening afternoon, looking for a name. A green light shone from a tall mast on top of its wheelhouse, a navigation signal indicating that the vessel was trawling. And it had an English name. "Arctic Storm," I called on the radio, "are you towing there?" "Roger, Roger," came the reply. "How do you want to pass?"

I was quite surprised to see an American factory trawler. Over the ensuing years, more American factory trawlers appeared and eventually foreign ships were pushed out entirely, ending our joint ventures. Some of the joint venture trawlers banded together to build at-sea processing platforms. They included a 668-foot long former container ship, the U.S.S. President Wilson, now renamed the Ocean Phoenix. These fleets continue the at-sea delivery methods used during the joint venture fisheries. Other boats take the catch aboard and use refrigerated seawater to keep it cool for delivery to a shore-side processing facility. The American Fisheries Act of 1998 codified and circumscribed the activities of these three groups of trawlers.

CHAPTER 23

CRABBING CONCERNS

A Fear of Fishing

During the heyday of king crab fishing, deckhands lined the dock vying for a chance to fish on a crab boat. It was common for a young man to offer to work for free—just for the experience, hoping to prove himself worthy of a share. But it is always risky to take an unknown person. Few have the courage, stamina, and the right amount of craziness, that defines a successful crab boat deckhand.

Clint was a farm hand from Idaho. Hoping a few years fishing the Bering Sea would provide the means to purchase a farm of his own, he ventured to Dutch Harbor. Powerfully built and with a resume of heavy labor including bucking hay bales and moving irrigation pipe, he seemed to have potential. Each time we pulled in to Dutch Harbor, Clint came to the boat to check for an opening. After the close of a king crab season, one of the deckhands had an emergency at home and left the boat. The three remaining deckhands were sufficient to pick up the last load of gear, but it seemed like a fine opportunity to give the persistent Clint a try. It would be a three-day trip, including one day traveling to the gear, one day hauling pots, and one day back to town. I promised Clint that if he worked hard and proved himself, I would take him salmon tendering that summer. He spent $300 on a commercial crew fishing license, boots, gloves, and raingear. He was thrilled to finally be on board.

An operating fishing boat can be a much different environment than the same boat tied to the dock. With engines running, pumps and motors humming, and waves pounding on the hull, the experience can be frightening to the uninitiated. The movement, of course, can be difficult, even sickening. But the weather was decent and the trip to the gear was easy and pleasant. Clint seemed to be handling the new situation well. Thirty minutes from the gear, I called the crew. Clint donned his raingear along with the rest of the men and followed them out on deck. Perhaps it was then that he realized he was not in Idaho anymore.

The deck on the Pacific Sun was wet, noisy and active. In the galley, there are things to hang on to and to help one stand and walk. On the deck, compensating for motion involves legwork, balancing, leaning, and feeling the pitch and roll of the boat. A deckhand needs to respond and adjust for the movement unconsciously. Something about the situation spooked Clint. As the pots started coming aboard, I couldn't see him with the deck camera. "Where is Clint?" I asked over the loudhailer.

"He's in the galley," a voice said. "He chickened out."

After four hours of hauling pots, a short run to another string of gear gave me the opportunity to speak with Clint. Duty, honor, self-respect, commitment, and pride—I ran down the list of reasons why he should at least try. "Most men are frightened at first," I explained. "But they get used to it. When you get back home, you will be disappointed that you didn't at least try." With that, he agreed to take another look. By that time, pots filled the deck all the way to the galley hatch. To get to the hauling area, he had to climb over a few pots. Veteran crab fishermen are adept at climbing up, down, and around on pots. They easily run across stacked pots, stepping on the steel bars of the pot frames.

Our pots were seven feet tall. Even short deckhands could grab the top bar, hop up on the center bar, and swing themselves to the top. They do it hundreds of times in a trip. But Clint didn't make it up his first pot. He lifted himself to the center bar and slipped off, cracking two ribs in the process. Back in Dutch Harbor, Clint didn't say goodbye. Before the boat was even fully tied to the dock, he was gone. From the wheelhouse, I watched him walk slowly down the dock carrying his bag and clutching his side, not once looking back. It was sad to see a good man so defeated by fear.

Tackled

Crab fishing has given many men an opportunity to face fears they may not have known they had. Bart was a large young man. He had no previous experience on crab boats but was eager to try and confident in his abilities. Two years earlier he played defensive tackle on his college's Pac-12 conference football team. Now graduated, he looked to crab fishing to give him a financial boost. As a tackle, Bart was accustomed to being knocked down and banged around, a part of crab fishing no duteous deckhand can avoid. Two essential qualities characterizing a good deckhand are a high tolerance for pain and the ability to take a punch dished out by Mother Nature. I thought a college football lineman would at least check those two boxes.

The weather was good when we got to the gear and started hauling. Bart learned quickly, and his strength and agility were assets. But Bart was afraid of bacon. We didn't have a designated cook, so I told the deckhands to take turns. Bart's turn came on the fourth day of the trip. He had no experience cooking but was willing to give it a try. Granted, cooking in a crab boat's galley can be considerably more complex than cooking at home. On a boat, it can be hard to stand up in a storm, but to stand up, boil potatoes, make a salad, and fry a steak is more than many people can manage. But Bart's first cooking day was calm and the stovetop was stable. He laid strips of bacon in a frying pan and turned on the heat. Soon the bacon started to sizzle, pop, and move. It was more than Bart bargained for. He darted from the galley hollering, "I can't do this! I can't do this!" Some people just aren't cut out for cooking.

As always happens, the weather changed. A gale kicked the seas up to fifteen or twenty feet in height. The seas were ordinary for the rest of us, but new for Bart. Yet, he seemed to be handling this new environment well. At least until a wave caught him crossing the deck and knocked him down. Being crushed by a very large wave is frightening and dangerous. Ice-cold water penetrates the raingear and instantly soaks and shocks. It fills the nostrils and stings the eyes. Disoriented and helpless, time warps into slow motion as questions explode in one's mind. Which way is up? Am I hurt? Will I be hurt? Is the boat going to sink? Am I on the boat or overboard? I have experienced both options. I once had to medevac a man whose leg was broken by an unfortunate fall after he was carried across the deck by a boarding sea. Hundreds of my own bad landings seem to hurt still today.

Bart, however, was not crushed by a large wave. He just floundered and fell over in a small sea that didn't cause any of the others on deck to even stumble. For Bart, the experience was worse than bacon. He ran to his cabin and locked the door. After giving him a few hours to relax and find inner strength, I tried offering encouragement through his stateroom door. But Bart was not interested in talking, and would not acknowledge or respond to any of my questions. He was done. Three days later we tied up in Dutch Harbor, and Bart disappeared without a word.

As a captain, I spent considerable time counseling greenhorns in the art of courage. Some responded favorably. Others, like Bart, were unwilling to be coached. Courage is confidence that comes from experience. It is awareness of the sea as well as the deck. Feeling the movement of the boat, hearing its sounds, and anticipating danger are all skills that contribute to courage. More of an intellectual process than a brave heart, courage on a crab deck is a fearless respect for surrounding conditions.

Becoming a Pirate

Crab feet are like spikes—and needle sharp at the tip. Not content to merely tear up my rain gear or perforate my boots, on October 16, 1980, a crab put its foot in my eye. It was quite painful. Dizziness was almost immediate. I went into shock. I worried about blindness. Blood infused the white of my eye. With my ratted hair and unshaven face, I was fearsome looking. The small laceration leaked fluid for a few hours.

The shock led to a weird hunger for fruit, and I ate three apples and two oranges. I applied antibiotic to the punctured eye, applied some gauze, and donned a black eye patch. The pirate jokes were insufferable. A headache persisted for three days. The eye eventually started to clear. I hoped the red would persist at least until I could frighten my kids, but by the time I returned home, I had nothing to show for the ordeal.

Liners

"Do you remember when I used to give you a hard time about wearing liners?" David asked.

"Of course," I replied. "I also remember when you claimed the rash on your arm was syphilis." We first met on the first American super-trawler, the Seafreeze Pacific, when I was fifteen. We worked together for several years after that as deckhands on the Paragon II. Now, thirty-five years later, I was the captain and David was a deckhand.

He apparently came to the wheelhouse to discuss gloves. "I was crazy," he said, holding up a hand covered in a clean white cotton glove liner. David and Arturo, two seasoned Portuguese fishermen, teased me relentlessly when I started wearing cotton liners under my neoprene fishing gloves. In their seasoned opinions, wearing liners under gloves was not sufficiently manly, or at least fishermanly.

Handling needle-covered king crab is hard on the hands, liners or not. Coiling line also was hurtful to hands due to the tight grip necessary to hold and manipulate the vibrating line. Sudden slips caused by knots bouncing in the block snapped the line like a whip, stinging the hands. In the heyday of king crab fishing, the thousands of crab handled, and thousands of lines coiled, caused me excruciating hand pain. Liners added a bit of padding and helped keep my hands warm. It was a small relief, but worth being ridiculed for.

After long hours on deck, sleep was appreciated, but waking was painful. Besides hurting all over from the beating one regularly takes on deck, coiling line caused hands to clench and spasm during sleep. Some fishermen covered their hands in lanolin (Bag Balm), slipped them into socks, and taped them over tennis balls. I tried it too, but it didn't seem to help.

As the season progressed, my hands became heavily calloused. Cracked fingertips (and even cracked and bloody palms) were worse than the pain from crab spine punctures. Lotions, creams, and oils soon washed off, leaving my broken skin exposed to hardening from the harsh salty environment. Often in the morning I would be unable to move my fingers. I soaked them in hot water, shook them vigorously, and held them over my head just to muster enough dexterity to dress. Once working, bodies and hands loosened up and functioned, but pain was part of a deckhand's life. Some fishermen used drugs to deal with the pain and fatigue of fishing. Many died because of it. I preferred the pain. Few things let you know you are alive like salt water on cracked hands.

Automatic line coilers were an innovation I never experienced as a deckhand. They eliminated the need for coiling, the most demanding and painful part of a deckhand's work. Coiling was a test of endurance and skill. It was the defining skill that set a full-share deckhand apart from a half-share man. Some deckhands are not quick or coordinated enough to coil. Most just lack experience. Today it is a lost art, and I am obsolete. I am happy though, and a bit jealous, that deckhands today do not have to experience what David and I did, with or without liners.

The Art of Coiling

"Coiling line is easy. I can do it no problem." The boast from a young deckhand sounded like a challenge.

"Have you coiled by hand before?" I asked.

"Nope, but it looks easy," he responded.

"Okay," I said, "let's see." When the mate came to relieve me, I donned raingear and gloves and headed to the deck.

To haul a pot, the captain maneuvers the boat close to the pot's two or three buoys. A deckhand throws a grappling hook, trying to catch the line between the buoys. He pulls the buoys to the boat and quickly lifts the line onto a grooved hydraulic power block. If he is too slow, the line will tighten and the buoys will be pulled off the deck causing angry comments from the captain. When the boat rises on a big sea, the buoy might need to be pinched off and held over the rail until the boat falls down again. Experienced deckhands know tricks for getting the buoy line in the block. Once the line is in the block, it hauls the rest of the buoy configuration on board and then quickly pulls up the 800-pound pot and any crab it may contain. Today, the line after the buoy set-up is run through a hydraulic coiler. Lacking a coiler, a deckhand grabs the line and coils it by hand. With the block running at full speed, a skilled coiler can create a reasonably formed pile of line that can be re-set without tangling.

I invited the confident deckhand to coil by hand. With the block running at half-speed, the line sprung uncooperatively across the deck, forming random curlicues and large loops. I stopped the block several times so the frustrated novice could rearrange the line into a semblance of a coil. It was a mess. I took the next pot, flipping the block speed control lever to full speed. When the pot surfaced, a perfect coil of line lay at my feet. "How did you do that?" the deckhand hollered.

"I've coiled thousands of pots by hand," I replied with a grin, "Thousands and thousands of pots." Then, just to show off, I coiled the next pot with one hand behind my back. "Thousands of pots," I reiterated, "Thousands."

Fishing on the Slime Bank

Crab boat deckhands particularly despise a king and bairdi crab fishing area north of Unimak Island from Cape Mordvinof to Otter Point. Called the Slime Bank, the moniker is a well-deserved reference to an abundance of slimy jellyfish inhabiting the area. The jellyfish of the species Chrysaora melanaster or Northern Sea Nettle grow to two feet across the bell, with smelly brown tentacles up to ten feet in length. The jellies wrap around and coat the buoy lines of pots. When the line is hauled, stinging cells from the tentacles are sprayed across the deck and into the eyes and faces of fishermen.

A crab pot buoy line typically includes a twenty-five or thirty-three fathom shot (length of line) made of sinking nylon line and a similar shot of floating polypropylene line. This arrangement keeps excess line from floating on the surface or settling on the bottom. It also keeps any excess line in the middle of the water column where it collects every jellyfish that passes. A knot connects the shots in the middle. The knot blocks jellyfish from sliding all the way down the line to the pot. They form a blob at the knot that can be two feet or more in diameter. At times, so many jellies collect in the knot blob, that it will lift the line out of the block and send the pot plummeting again to the bottom of the sea. An alert deckhand must quickly throw the line out of the coiler, toss some slack overboard and then try to get it back in the block. This must be done without being pulled overboard and drowning in jellyfish-infested waters.

To avoid this problem, the block is stopped at the knot, and the jellyfish are cut away with a knife. When the pot surfaces, it is also covered with the same stinging brown slime. As the pot is lifted aboard, toxic threads blow menacingly in the wind like a thousand whips of stinging snot. Slippery jellyfish pour from the pot, cover the deck, and help cushion the falls they cause. Brown goo finds its way everywhere. It coats beards, covers raingear, and reaches into nostrils, stinging as it goes.

Tentacles attack everyone's eyes. Goggles don't work. The brown goo quickly coats them. Wiping the stinging slime from the eyes is a mistake. Touching stimulates a hundred more stinging cells to toss their barbed harpoons into the eyes and sensitive surrounding skin. Stumbling to the crab tank and flinging handfuls of salt water into the distressed eyeball is the only way to find relief.

Crab fishing is not the only fishery afflicted by the jellyfish. Trawls are hauled back dripping with them and I have watched seiners showered by the brownish blobs. The Sea Nettle is found throughout the Bering Sea. I have no idea why or how they concentrate in certain places, but they are a bane to fishermen who invade their domain.

Crew Concerns

Before fishing, Mike was in the U.S. Army. He became a Ranger, and served as a sniper in various covert operations in Central America. His maturity, discipline, and experience made him an ideal choice to run the deck. Mike gave instructions when necessary. Commands are part of an orderly deck, not a matter of being overbearing or a product of a military background. With new deckhands, it's the responsibility of the most experienced deckhands, especially one acting as a deck boss, to insure the safety of others, and to help the greenhorn learn.

Given the active and dangerous environment, there is usually little time for explanation and discussion. Much of a greenhorns instruction in the finer points of crab fishing is delivered at a high volume, often with angry tones, and punctuated by profanity. In my greenhorn crab season, instructions were also frequently followed by a physical reminder of my incompetence. If I was not quick enough completing a task, the deck boss would push me roughly out of the way—sometimes with a sharp elbow to my chest—and finish the job himself.

Most deckhands understand that captain's orders are to be obeyed immediately and without question. It is done without needing to know why. But the position of the deck boss is more familiar and therefore less respected. Depending on the dynamic of the deck, a designated boss may or may not be necessary. Some crews don't need one. Some of my most enjoyable seasons as a deckhand were spent with guys so experienced and familiar with each other that actions could be anticipated and needs recognized and met without words.

Dave lacked maturity, discipline, and experience, but he was smart, young, and energetic. Mike and Dave made a great team most of the time. But Dave was ambitious and arrogant. He discovered that Mike could sometimes be mistaken, and perceived fallibility as a vulnerable underbelly inviting attack.

Some years, I reserved percentage points (most fishing crews are paid a percentage of revenues) to be awarded as bonuses after the season. The bonus is supposed to incentivize effort, but instead it often spawned subterfuge. Best friends would reveal their shipmates darkest secrets trying for a few more pennies at no extra effort. Much of the backstabbing was pathetically transparent, but some creative deckhands executed expert and entertaining attempts to gain preeminence. Preludes might include subtle innuendos with mock apprehensions of returning mental health issues or tales of personal problems that were detracting from a deckhand's work. Over the weeks, expressed concerns carefully escalated. Finally, the prevaricator reported criticisms of the captain, violations of vessel rules, or mental instability. He may explain how hard it has been for him to pick up the slack from the other's slothfulness.

As the season drew to a close, Dave increasingly sought to undermine Mike's authority in a quest for a higher percentage. His visits to the wheelhouse were sure to include information on the latest of Mike's errors, his laziness, or his incompetence. I was amused at his patently amateur approach to artifice. Dave skipped the foundation and went directly to the end game. I was not amused.

Frustrated at his failure to get Mike fired, and seething at each subsequent order, Dave finally went terminal and took a swing at Mike's jaw. He missed. It's never a good idea to swing at a soldier, especially a Spec Ops Soldier. When Dave woke up, he might have been okay for the one trip remaining in the season, but there was a no-fight policy on the boat, and I had to enforce it. He packed his gear and left the boat, earning a substantial penalty in pay.

Dirty Crab

Every new crab fishery and every new area has a learning curve. I saw an occasional opilio while fishing king crab, but the fishery didn't develop until after I was well ensconced in the captain's chair. So my first snow crab season involved a lot of guessing. Knowing nothing, I found a spot where several other boats were fishing and laid out some strings. The Pelagos had three crab tanks and packed around 220,000 pounds of snow crab. Surprisingly, the tanks started quickly filling with the feisty beige crab. When the count per pot started to drop off, I moved a few miles. The crabs in the new area were ugly. The undersides, usually creamy white, were covered with grotesque blotches of dark brown. The top of the shell was similarly mottled. Many shells carried small cities of barnacles and sprouts of seaweed.

Some king crab come with black spots and barnacles too. In my early days on deck, there was plenty of clean king crab, so the ugly ones were returned to the sea, suffering only the agony of rejection. Later, as king crab became scarce, every crab was beautiful, barnacles or not. We didn't discriminate. The crew wanted to know what to do. Should they toss the ugly crab in the tank or send them out the trash chute? I didn't know, and asking someone over the radio would reveal my amateur status to the entire fleet. That wouldn't work. I thought there must be a market for them somewhere; after all, the meat tastes the same, it's just the packaging that's not pretty. And it seemed a shame to work so hard hauling gear for nothing. I told the crew to throw the ugly bugs into the aft tank and stack the pots on deck. I moved to another area, found more attractive crab and filled the boat.

We offloaded to a processing ship anchored off St. Paul Island. They loved the crab in the first two tanks, but when we pumped down the aft tank with the discolored crab, their mood soured. They were not interested in purchasing the unusually decorated crab at any price. I called around to some of the other processors in the neighborhood. The response was disappointing. They all refused the off-color crab. Some thought it highly amusing that I kept them. The best offer I found was "We are happy to lend you a brailer that you may return them to mother nature." Chagrined, I kept the crab on board. In a few days, the boat was full again. This time, I ran to Dutch Harbor to offload.

The forward tanks of clean, beautiful crab were offloaded first. But as the hatch cover of the aft hatch was removed, the offloaders looked confused. I watched the dock for the superintendent to appear, bracing myself for some bad news. It didn't take long. "Jake," he said, "What's with the dirty crab?" I mumbled something stupid. "Well," he said, "I can't pay you full price for it." The full price was $0.75 per pound (crab went cheap in those days).

"That's terrible news," I sighed. "How much can you give me for them?" He thought for a moment and offered me $0.55. "Oh," I responded sadly, trying hard to conceal my delight, "the meat is just as good as any other crab, but I understand your position. I agree." The offloaders climbed in the tank and went to work. I didn't keep any more dirty crab after that.

CHAPTER 24

OBSERVATIONS

Fisheries Observers

Many fisheries in the United States (and around the world) require all or some participating vessels to carry observers. The information amassed by observers is part of sustainability science and used in fisheries management. Most fisheries observers are fine professionals dedicated to the difficult task of data collection on a fishing boat. The stories I relate below are exceptions. They tell of isolated experiences with a few individuals during the early days of observer activity in Alaska and are extracted from a much broader and overall positive experience with observers. While the stories are accurate, names have been changed and boat names omitted. I am not trying to get anyone in trouble, especially myself. My purpose is to convey the realities of my limited and unique fishing experience.

Decades ago, I related some of these stories to the Commissioner of the Alaska Department of Fish and Game at a meeting covering observer issues. He became agitated and demanded to know why I did not immediately report the incidents to authorities. "Next time you notice you are speeding," I suggested, "Call the highway patrol and request a citation." I think he got my point. Returning to port to replace an observer costs valuable fishing time, increases expenses and creates the potential for legal problems. It wasn't worth it. We never intentionally violated fishing regulations, but undersize crab or species that should be discarded, occasionally end up (illegally) in the hopper. I would rather have the crew correct a problem than have a fisheries observer document and report the problem to law enforcement. So if an observer is lazy, incompetent or otherwise unable or unwilling to perform their duties, who am I to complain?

Ben

How many Louie L'amore novels can an observer read during a snow crab season? That was Ben's concern. It was cold and dangerous on deck. He got crab asthma in the factory. He had to get through chapter five. These excuses justified the sampling technique of "guessing from the wheelhouse." From his perch on the port side of the pilothouse, Ben recorded his observations. "Looks like four-hundred legal opilio, ten females, three codfish, and a basket star," he opined as he recorded the figures in his data book. "Nobody looks at this," he assured me. Ben was an experienced observer with several years observing in a number of different fisheries. Not once, in the five months he sailed with us, did I see him set foot in our factory or pick up a crab.

Dave

Dave was different. He spent hours on deck and in the factory. He sorted and measured crab, packed the sections into baskets, and helped when he saw an opportunity. More than anything, Dave wanted to be accepted and appreciated by the crew and would not dream of reporting a violation. He was hard at work sorting through piles of crab when complaints started coming from the factory. The butchers were finding sub-legal sized crab in the hopper. Small crab in a box devalues the product. Since the crew worked on a percentage basis, we wanted to get the most we could for a box of crab. We did not want sub-legal crab and we did not keep them.

The factory foreman noticed small crab appearing whenever Dave was sorting. When he left, the small crab problem stopped. Bemused and a bit bewildered, the foreman reported to me that the observer was throwing the prohibited catch in the hopper. I had a discussion with Dave. I gave him a movie player and a pile of videos and asked him to carefully review each one as many times as necessary. It kept him busy for the rest of the season.

A few years later, Dave was assigned to sail with me again. He was now using a different name. It was an oddly accented variation of the name he used previously. I asked him up front to please not help us sort crab. With that understood, he was a pleasure to have on board. He was entertaining, helpful, and always gave us an opportunity to correct any problems he found. Most of the time we offloaded product to cargo ships (trampers) around the Pribilof Islands. Eventually, we needed fuel and set course for Dutch Harbor. Dave set course straight for the bar. When we were ready to leave, Dave was not on board. We searched the bars, inquired at the hotel, and checked with the police. He was reported urinating in a phone booth the day before, but no one we asked had seen him since. Perhaps he fell into the water, trying to board the boat late at night. Maybe a Samaritan had given him a place to sleep until he sobered up. Crews scoured the city searching for the missing man. After six hours he was finally found. He was asleep in a dumpster.

There are female observers as well. While I was off-shift and asleep, the mate was at the wheel. The weather was rough, and a boarding sea hit one of the deckhands. After the season, he sued the boat claiming he was injured in the incident. He claimed that his injury would not have occurred if the mate had been paying attention and alerted him to the oncoming wave. In the course of examination, it was determined that at the time of the injury the observer was performing fellatio on the first mate. Apparently everyone on the boat knew this was going on, except for me.

Harold

Harold was a new observer, fresh out of the training program. He was young, energetic, and idealistic. It was clear that he relished his capacity as a quasi-enforcement official, determined to defend mother earth from nefarious fishermen like me. He had no authority to issue tickets for violations, but he could report violations to authorities. And he seemed far too eager to do so.

Because of the way the deck was arranged, our operation was one of the cleanest in the fleet. Certainly no violations were intentional, but occasionally a sub-legal or female crab (also not legal) will attach to a legal crab and end up in the hopper. They are removed by the butcher and returned to the sea, but any illegal crab in the hopper is a violation. Experienced observers know that these accidents happen. They may remove the accidental crab without comment, or watch to see how the situation is handled. Fair observers give the crew a chance to correct any problems they find.

A few weeks into the trip, Harold finally saw his opportunity. He found a slightly sub-legal crab in the hopper. Excitedly, he bounded up the wheelhouse ladder and pulled the camera from his observer case. "What are you doing Harold?" I asked.

"I found a small crab. I have to document it," he replied gleefully.

Enraged, I shouted "What? There was a small crab in the hopper?"

"Yes" replied Harold, shocked by my sudden animation.

I put the boat into a wide turn and opened the throttle to full speed. Grabbing the microphone for the deck loudhailer, I started screaming. "I told you guys that no illegal crab was ever to enter the hopper. That's it. You can't do that on my boat. We are going to Dutch Harbor, and you are all fired. Do you hear me? All of you are fired!" Harold turned white. "I, I, I guess I don't have to document," he stammered weakly. Turning to address him directly, I pointedly replied "No. You. Don't!" Harold put the camera back in its case.

Had he gone to the other side of the wheelhouse and looked aft, he would have seen the deckhands working undisturbed, sorting crab and getting ready for the next pot. I had not pressed the loudhailer microphone's transmit button. The only one who heard my rant was Harold. The rest of the season went well. I never heard from Harold after that season, but I hope he spent time on other crab boats so he could appreciate what a clean operation we had.

CHAPTER 25

THE GALLEY GOURMET

Cooking on a Boat

Food is second only to making money as a contributor to shipboard morale. My father believed that since food was the only physical pleasure available to fishermen, only the best food would do. He bought expensive cuts of meat from a butcher shop, the best ice cream, cheeses, and jams. Heavenly bread and exquisite pastries came from a local Norwegian bakery. But purchasing expensive ingredients does not guarantee good food.

My grandfather owned and operated restaurants for much of his life. When he sailed as the cook on the Paragon, palate-pleasing food was always provided. But many boat cooks have unusual interpretations of culinary competence. Roy, the fat, greasy, toothless cook that replaced Granddad for a summer, coated lettuce with mayonnaise and called it salad. He covered both sides of a bread slice with a heavy coating of salt, singed it on the griddle and titled it toast. He explained that salt was necessary to keep the bread from sticking to the iron griddle. A simple experiment demonstrated his misunderstanding, but did not persuade him to cut the crusty sodium from his recipe.

Jim, a temporary cook on the Paragon II, concocted a failed mimic of macaroni and cheese. Boiled elbow macaroni was mixed with cubes of brown Norwegian Gjetost cheese. Its unique earthy flavor (think dirt) is repulsive to most Americans, but my father liked it. The mixture was covered with Green Goddess salad dressing (like Ranch dressing only green). I didn't try it. Jim didn't try it either. It went over the side.

Later in the trip, we were hauling pots and the captain sent Jim to the galley to prepare a quick lunch. He was gone for an hour while we worked short-handed. When lunch was finally ready, we found that Jim placed a pound of Nabob raspberry jam in a skillet and cut hot dogs into coins, carefully simmering the concoction as he sat patiently in the galley waiting for the flavors to blend. I made a sandwich. The other deckhands did likewise. No one tried the hotdog jam. This not-so-clever creation was also consigned to the sea.

A different deckhand's attempt at stroganoff resulted in an enormous pot of a thin gray liquid into which he added strips of pimento loaf. I did not try it. He substituted pimento loaf for beef because he thought it would thaw faster. He replaced a typical sour cream stroganoff sauce with a thin gray liquid because he had no idea how to make stroganoff and apparently couldn't consult the cookbook. That too was donated to Davy Jones's diner.

Of course, not all boat food is disgusting. Two of my cooks were certified and experienced chefs. One owned a Seattle restaurant for two decades. The other worked as a chef at an upscale Seattle eatery. We ate well the years they were with us. On smaller boats the cook is typically a deckhand who may or may not have any prior experience cooking. As a general observation, the most egregious gustatory insults occur on crab catcher boats, probably because there is often so little time for cooking. On many occasions, the evening meal was a microwaved burrito fed to me by another deckhand while I coiled line.

Competent cooks were in short supply in the crab fleet due to the rarity of persons capable of cooking and competent on deck. On some boats each crewmember contributed to paying a dedicated cook. My sister Nancy worked as the cook on both the Paragon and Paragon II. She made life on a boat bearable.

I also took a turn or two at cooking, once while I was also deck boss and engineer. I preferred to prepare as much as possible in port, freezing the meals so I didn't have to spend more time off the deck than was necessary. When eating in shifts, the cook eats last. This eating strategy trains the cook to prepare a sufficient quantity for everyone. My wife continues to complain that I cook too much food.

Whether as a deckhand on a smaller boat or a dedicated cook feeding a hundred hungry mouths on a factory trawler, anyone with aspirations of cooking on a boat should consider the significant challenges posed by the often-hostile environment of the Bering Sea. Cooking appliances on boats range from the stove tops, ovens, and refrigerators commonly found in a home kitchen to commercial products for food service. But all must be modified for use at sea. Latches and cords keep doors closed. Stovetops are fit with movable grids that hold pans in place. Cardboard box containers limit sliding in the refrigerator. Tin cans with one end flattened insert into the oven rack to hold pans in place. Most fishing boats maintain a supply of blackened half-crushed cans for the oven.

These modifications are not always effective. Sometimes a sharp jolt from a sudden sea will spring a poorly designed refrigerator latch and release the contents to decorate the deck like a Jackson Pollock painting, or a chicken, sprung from the oven, will range freely across the floor. Rough weather can open cabinets and drawers, and distribute their contents in a cacophony of clangs and clatters. Liquid in a pan stays level while the boat does not. This interesting fact of physics results in spills and smoke filled galleys and is the bane of boat cooks. When waters are rough, smart cooks prepare a pizza. They save the soup for more serene seas.

Cooking is repulsive to a person with motion sickness. My personal experience with seasickness was confined to childhood, but the associated smell of coffee continues to conjure up nauseating nostalgia, causing me to avoid the grocery store coffee aisle to this day. On the other hand, cooks unaffected by stormy seas cheerfully prepare sumptuous food that is ignored by queasy crewmen.

Dirty Sock Sole

Joe served as an officer in the Cambodian army during the conflict in Vietnam and came to the United States as a refugee escaping the Khmer Rouge. He had some previous fishing experience in California, but it was his first time in the Bering Sea. We were trawling for flatfish, but the cook never prepared them. Hungry for fish, Joe asked which of the fish we caught was the best to eat. "The sock sole," he was told, "One of these." The deckhand handed Joe the fish. Later that day, Joe cooked and—much to our surprise—ate the fish.

When cooked, the flat fish smells and tastes like well-worn unwashed socks. Joe's frying filled the galley with the pungent smell of stinky feet and garlic. Joe dined on the smelly fish every day for a week and we could no longer stand the stench. It was finally suggested that he might like yellowfin sole, a delicious fish, even better than the sock-flavored flounder. Fortunately, he did.

The Missing List

During a season on the Pelagos, the cook had to leave for a meeting with his parole officer. While at sea it was not possible to adequately communicate with authorities, and he was being threatened with re-incarceration. My entire crew that year were ex-convicts or parolees, and a few had similar problems. Dan, another of the deckhands, agreed to be the cook. Dan did an excellent job. The meals were well balanced, tasteful, and satisfying. On the way to Dutch Harbor with a load of crab to deliver, I asked him to prepare an inventory and shopping list so we could re-supply. In town, I asked Dan for his list. He admitted he had not made one. "What?" I exclaimed angrily, "you had all day yesterday. What is wrong with you?" I demanded to know. Dan sat quietly on the edge of his bunk, saying nothing. He stared into the bulkhead in front of him. Tears formed on his work-hardened cheeks. "Oh no," I said, suddenly feeling awful as a few previous incidents jelled into a realization. "You can't read can you?"

"No," he replied, his gaze shifting to the deck.

"I am so sorry," I said, feeling his hurt and regretting my reprimand. Together we sorted through the groceries and made the food order. I was impressed with how well he cooked without recipes or reading. But then, people have been doing it for tens of thousands of years.

How Fishermen Eat

Walking through a restaurant frequented by fishermen, you may observe people wrapping their left arm around the top of their plate, often while the left-hand tightly grips a glass. They are fishermen, securing their dinner from sliding across the table. Even with the ever-present green mesh galley tablemat (now also available in other colors), fishermen hold their plates. They may also eat rapidly, unconsciously anxious to get back on deck, or up to the wheel-house. Gentle reminders of "Jake, you are not on the boat anymore," betray my wife's embarrassment at taking me out in public.

CHAPTER 26

STORIES OF LOVE, LIFE, AND BOMBERS

Drugs on Boats

Dutch Harbor in the early 1970s was an unusual experience for a seventeen-year-old from a conservative religious home. Kids I knew in high school smoked pot and took pills, but I never saw heroin use until I came to Dutch Harbor. At the processing plant where I lived and worked, drugs of all kinds were easily obtained, and openly used. A lone Alaska State Trooper lived on the Unalaska side of town, and the only way to the Dutch Harbor side (on a different island) was by skiff or the tiny ferry "Islander." He rarely came over, and when he did it was usually in response to a crime of violence. The drug trade flourished, and few seemed to care. Drugs flowed on fishing boats as well. The boats I worked on were clean, but others were known drug boats. In the late 1970s, during the heyday of king crab fishing, boats were met at the dock by drug dealers and prostitutes, all wanting to cash in on a share of the lucrative season. There was little or no interference in these activities by law enforcement. The police didn't hesitate, however, to wake me up at 2:00 a.m. to issue a citation for leaving the sodium fishing lights on.

I did not allow drugs (or alcohol) on any of my boats, but some captains dispensed cocaine like candy. I never needed it to stay competitive. I worked for days without sleep, and without crystal meth. I don't even drink coffee. Drug use is responsible for many of the lives lost in the Bering Sea, and wiser boat owners actively enforce the zero tolerance policy required by law.

Today, drug use among fishermen continues to be a problem. But testing programs and enforcement activities keep it in the realm of whispers and dark corners. Dealers no longer openly peddle their product on the docks of Dutch Harbor. Still, drug use remains as pervasive as in any sector of society, and takes a terrible toll on the lives and health of many fishermen and their families.

The Bear Bomber

The radar picked up a large target, approaching very fast from the west. It could only be an airplane. It was unusual for the radar to detect aircraft in the middle of the North Pacific as they are usually too high. Coast Guard C-130s sometimes patrol these waters, but typically they stay within the two-hundred-mile zone, and we were well outside, in international waters.

I soon spotted visually what the radar reported. A long black streak was approaching my position, and it was flying very low. As it passed overhead, I could see that it was not a C-130. This one had swept wings. The wings on a C-130 are straight. Red stars painted beneath each wing were clearly visible, as were the weird double propellers on each engine. A Russian bear bomber just buzzed us! The huge plane flew several miles to the east and then began a slow turn, circling until it lined up with us again. As it approached, I wondered what I should do if the bomb bay doors opened or the cannons lit up. Fortunately, the bomb bay doors remained closed and the guns stayed quiet. The deadly plane passed over with a roar and disappeared beyond the horizon. Thoughts of vulnerability occupied my watch. They could have easily destroyed us and who would know? We would have been just another vessel that vanished at sea.

Love One Another

I met the Love Family (a communal hippie group) in 1975. My father hated hippies. That much was clear. The hippie movement spawned many communitarian social experiments. One such movement in the Seattle area was The Love Family, also known as the Church of Jesus Christ at Armageddon.

Founded by Paul Erdman—also known as Israel Love (or Love Israel)—as a religious hippie community, they purchased a three hundred acre farm and some businesses, and began to prosper. In 1975 they acquired a fishing boat named Kathy Jo, and optimistically renamed it Abundance. Built in Tacoma,

WA in 1942, the Abundance first served in the U.S. Navy as a minesweeper. It was decommissioned in 1946 and converted to a fishing vessel in 1947.

I first heard of the Love Family from my father. There was nothing about them that met with his approval. So I was surprised to find my father helping out with their dilapidated old boat. Captain Courage Israel and his crew had little experience on boats and even less experience fishing.

Over the months of preparation for fishing, my father helped the hippies in their new venture. They had little money, even for necessities. My father gave them gear, parts, and whatever else they needed. He sometimes instructed me to go to the galley, prepare a box of food, and deliver it to the Abundance. He could not tolerate hard working people going without sufficient food, even if they had long hair. He sold them one of his very expensive nets. The terms were simple—pay when you can.

When their boat was ready, they followed the Paragon II out of the Strait of Juan de Fuca and to the fishing grounds. They set their net where my father advised and hauled it back at his suggestion. Over the months of fishing, they were our shadow.

It was several years before the Paragon II again trawled off the coast of Washington, and I lost track of the Abundance. I don't know how long Courage and his crew fished, but years later a letter came in the mail. It was from Israel Love. Along with a letter of gratitude, he sent a check for the net they purchased, paid in full, with interest.

My father is a hard man. He does not display the softer emotions. But as he read the kind words and held the check in his hand, tears formed in his eyes and escaped across his cheeks; something I had never seen before or since. My father didn't need the money. By this time, he was a prosperous Bering Sea fisherman with two large steel crab boats. The check meant more than money. It was a token of integrity and thanks from people he loved and selflessly served, hippies.

The Order of Life

Flying fish are a phenomenon one has to see to believe. They come in a cloud, like locust on the sea, leaping from the surface to soar momentarily, splash down, and fly again. They make no effort to avoid the boat and hundreds end up on the deck, helplessly waving their little fins in a futile effort to regain flight. Where are they going and why? Is a team of hungry tuna pursuing them?

On the stern of the Paragon, while gazing in calm water illuminated by a shaft of sunlight, I saw a herring swim hurriedly by. A salmon was hot on its tail. A shark pursued the salmon. It was a real-life cartoon and a vivid reminder of the order of life. Every living animal tries to eat and avoid being eaten.

Voices in the night

Dutch Harbor can be ghostly quiet at 3:00 a.m. on those rare occasions when the wind is not blowing. While rigging gear in the crisp chill of early morning it was quiet enough to carry a faint call for help over the harbor. Unsure as to the direction of the call, I started quickly and quietly walking down the dirt road, straining to hear any sliver of sound. The next dock was about two hundred yards away. As I approached, I could hear splashing. A small processing ship was tied at the end of the dock. An older man, quite drunk, had fallen between the dock and the boat as he tried to board.

Finding a piece of nylon crab line, I formed a lasso. From the dock, it was about ten feet down to the water. I dropped the loop over the soggy sailor and pulled it tight. He was too heavy for me to lift alone, so hoisting him up enough to prevent drowning; I tied the line off to a cleat and ran for help. Together, three of us managed to haul him to the dock. We woke several of his shipmates, and they got him onto his boat and started treatment for hypothermia.

A few years later I pulled another man from the water. This time, it was daylight, and the man was sober enough to grab and hold a ring buoy while I pulled him to the shore. Both men were fortunate that the weather was calm. When the wind screams over the island, it is the only scream that is audible.

A Note on Albatross

Nothing avian is quite as amusing as albatross. Competing with comparatively sleek seagulls, speedy Murres, and agile petrels, survival of the several albatross species, although currently threatened, is a miracle. Albatross are the geeks of the sea.

A drifting gull just lifts its wings to the wind, and soars effortlessly from sea to sky. It lands with precision and grace, even in a storm, instantly transitioning between modes of travel. An albatross takes flight only after an awkward sprint across the sea, frequently failing in the attempt. And landing is equally cumbersome. With wings held high and feet fully extended, they hit the water with an ungainly splash. Once down, the ritualistic folding of the wings appears woefully uncoordinated. But in the air, the albatross seems to float effortlessly; completely competent and comfortable in the element it was created to command.

And Other Birds

Birds that have no business in the middle of the sea sometimes stop to rest on the boat. Some stay for only a few minutes. Others are utterly exhausted and require weeks of rest and recovery. My longest avian visitor was a young owl. It set down aft my wheelhouse and was all but dead. I took him inside and placed him on a towel in a cardboard box. After a days rest, he ate some fish. For five days he recuperated in my wheelhouse, eating fish and gaining strength. When I thought he was ready, I placed him in a shorter box and moved him just outside the wheelhouse door in an area that was warmer and protected, but still open if he decided to leave. He stayed another week, fattening on fish eagerly accepted from my fingers. When he finally took flight, it was a sad and happy day. I wonder how many birds, unable to find a boat, fall exhausted into the sea and perish.

Another owl stayed only for a few hours. A majestic adult snowy owl stood atop our crane through a nighttime blizzard. On the deck below, the crew was hauling pots and using the crane to stack them on deck. The owl watched dispassionately. He maintained his perch despite the rane's movement and the crashes and clatter of crab fishing. Just after daybreak he flew off, quickly disappearing in the falling snow.

Charters

Fishing boats sometimes pick up odd jobs called charters. A boat might spend time removing trash from Hawaiian reefs, serving as a support vessel for oil spill abatement, or conducting fisheries or oceanographic research. For me, charters were an interesting and relaxing diversion from the drudgery and stress of fishing. I enjoyed the company of biologists and fisheries scientists, and found their research endeavors fascinating.

Passed into law in 1976, the Magnuson-Stevens Fishery Conservation and Management Act provided for funding fishery resource assessments in the Bering Sea. As part of that effort, I was involved in a charter trawling at designated stations in the Bering Sea and as far north as the Bering Strait (from which we really could see Russia). We used a diminutive sampling trawl with tiny trawl doors. It was like playing with toys.

Four biologists sorted through and documented the catch from each tow. They took samples and cut the otoliths from the heads of flatfish. Otoliths are paired bone-like structures of calcium carbonate that float in a gelatinous mass behind the brains of bony fish. In fish, they facilitate the senses of hearing and balance. Humans have two analogous otolithic organs in each of their ears, the utricle and the saccule, which keep us gravitationally oriented. With growth rings similar to those of trees, fish otoliths can be used to determine age, which is why the biologists were so intent on extracting them from the poor sole's flat heads.

Around St. Lawrence Island, we pulled up tens of thousands of tiny snow crab. The biologists dutifully set about counting each cute little crab. Concerned for the crab as well as the biologists, I suggested they count how many crab fit into a basket and then count the baskets as they returned the tiny crab to the sea. That method worked out much better for the biologists and ensured the survival of many more crab.

Relationships

The day after returning from my honeymoon, I flew to Dutch Harbor to go crab fishing. Four months later, I arrived home to a tepid reception from my new bride. Who is this strange man, my wife wondered? She eventually warmed, and later reunions became easier. Somewhere through the years of absence and uncertainty, she became reconciled with the fact that she married a fisherman and her life would be different. Most of all, she grew to be flexible. She learned to experience happiness from emotional proximity instead of physical location. Along the way, she became a La Leche Leader, lactation consultant, midwife, and owner of a children's clothing store. She also raised our six children. The children were affected by my long disappearances as well. As a toddler, my oldest daughter was particularly angry at my absences. It would be several days after returning home before she would speak to me or allow me to hold her.

Most of my fishing was done before cell phones and satellites. Ship to shore radio, on which anyone could eavesdrop, made it difficult to discuss private matters. In Dutch Harbor, I sometimes walked several miles to find a phone booth, only to find it inoperable. But with sufficient effort we were usually able to converse. We both wrote many letters as well. Communicating was not always easy. When there were problems at home her pleas to quit fishing were compelling but impractical.

My wife came to visit me on the boat one year. Our first child was a breast-feeding toddler and stayed with grandma. It was September of 1980 when she flew into Dutch Harbor. I was trawling for pollock with the Pelagos in a joint venture with Korean processors. She caught a ride on a small trawler named Wild Mary. The weather was sloppy, and the Wild Mary was wild indeed. My wife lost her dinner to seasickness and had a miserable trip.

I was counting on the Koreans to use their thirty-foot workboat to transfer my wife from the Wild Mary to the Pelagos. At first they refused, but my brother, who was running another trawler in the venture and speaks fluent Korean, came on the radio. I have no idea what was said, but soon the workboat was in the water and heading to the Wild Mary. It was rough alongside the Pelagos. Perched on the bow of the workboat, my wife came up on a swell, where I caught her and lifted her aboard. She stayed on board as we finished the joint venture, converted the boat for crab fishing, and made our first trip of the king crab season. But she underestimated how difficult two weeks without her baby would be and was happy to return home.

I was not always able to give warning when I had a chance to come home. I frightened her late one night by knocking loudly on our front door. Once I was able to fly home for a short stay and was unable to contact her. I arrived in Seattle on a Saturday morning. I knew our son had an art lesson at the zoo on Saturday mornings, so I caught a cab to the zoo and waited at the entrance. Would she recognize her bedraggled husband in tattered boat clothes, with shoulder-length hair and a bushy beard? She did. And she picked me up!

Without being able to count on a reliable schedule, she planned family vacations per her convenience, and told me when she was leaving. Sometimes I made it, other times not. She once picked me up at the airport on her way out of town. And there were times I left the family somewhere and flew to Alaska.

Relationships are difficult to manage for fishermen. Companions become discouraged by the long absences and erratic pay, and they worry about the danger their loved one lives with. For many, the loneliness and uncertainty become too much to bear and they move on. I was blessed to marry a woman with independence, self-reliance, and the tenacity of a barnacle. Despite frequent disappointment, she endured.

A friend who produced the precursor to "Deadliest Catch" called "America's Deadliest Season: Alaskan Crab Fishing" once observed that crab fishermen tended to be people who were incapable of functioning in normal society. Her observation has merit. I left all my problems, challenges, and responsibilities at the dock. While at sea, I focused on fishing and bringing my boat and crew home safely. When I came home, it was clear the family functioned well without me. Their lives flew by as if on a carousel, and I watched, hoping to get on but not finding an opportunity. Except for providing money, I often felt irrelevant.

When I came home for a break, my wife still had to work, tending the affairs of the family and getting the kids to their games, lessons, and activities. She often felt slighted by the fact that I was free, and she was subject to a congested schedule. Somehow we pushed past the difficulties, heartache, and disappointments. If I am anything, it is because of the strength and determination of my wife. Without her I am adrift and lost.

When I was small, I wanted to make a present for my mother. I wanted her to have something beautiful. In my mind's eye was a sculpture of a seal. It was snowy white with brown spots on its back and had shiny black eyes and a small black nose. I took a knife from the kitchen drawer, unwrapped a new bar of soap, and began carving my seal. Soon I had a pile of shavings and a pitiful piece of soap that looked nothing like the animal I had envisioned. Some people realize their dreams. They have the correct tools for carving. They possess the skill necessary to bring their visions, hopes, and plans into reality. Despite my desire, I fell far short of my dreams for my wife, my children, and myself. I wanted to be so much more and give so much more than I was able. In the end, I was relevant primarily as a provider and sometimes struggled there. I came and went in the background, often unnoticed. My life is no work of art, but I tried to make it a work of love. I spent myself at sea for my family. I hated being away, but as my friend observed, I failed to function in normal society.

CHAPTER 27

WEATHER WOES

Working in the Rain

An acquaintance once asked if I was required to work in the rain. She had no idea that rain was the least of a fisherman's water worries. Working in foul weather is not always smart, but it is not something from which Bering Sea fishermen typically shy away. A prudent captain balances profit with patience, knowing the capacities of his crew and ship, as well as his own ability. An injured man or damaged boat will cost more than a few hours of waiting for a storm to subside, and no paycheck is worth the price of a life lost.

Rough weather risks are greatest in crab fishing. The crew is more exposed to the elements and working with heavy steel crab pots is inherently dangerous even in calm weather. Working through gales usually went without question. When winds blew over fifty knots, with thirty or forty-foot seas, it depended on the situation. As a captain, if I deemed the weather workable, I often left the decision to the experienced deckhands. After all, they were the ones most at risk. But I also knew that the bravado that brings them back to the Bering Sea would not allow them to refuse. A full-share deckhand's pride prevents him from shrinking before a storm. I knew it well. Frequently as a deckhand I stood in the wheelhouse surveying a tortured seascape, hearing the howled threats of a savage storm as I considered the same question posed by my captain, "Are you willing to work in this weather?" I could never say no. It is not in our nature.

Of course, some people have a greater sense of self-preservation that I apparently did. During a typical winter storm as the crew prepared for work, a greenhorn whose previous fishing experience was in summer salmon fishing came to the wheelhouse with tears streaming down his ruddy cheeks. "I can't do this," he cried pathetically. "I didn't realize the weather would be this bad."

"This isn't that bad," I explained in a tone devoid of tact. "It gets a lot worse." He quit.

Peggy

Few things are as important to fishermen as the weather. We plan our trips, manage our days, and make our decisions in consideration of the forecast. In the old days, Peggy Dyson, broadcasting on 4125 MHz from WBH29 Kodiak read the marine weather forecasts twice daily. Everyone listened to Peggy. Her name was synonymous with the weather report. If someone asked, "What does Peggy say?" everyone knew they were inquiring about the weather. She became our mom away from mom, and her familiar voice connected and comforted us through trying times.

Peggy's husband Oscar was a crab fisherman. In 1974, Peggy radioed Oscar and read the weather reports to him. Other fishermen tuned in to listen during their radio schedules. Later that year, she contracted with the National Weather Service to read the reports on a regular basis. She did so for twenty-five years. She conveyed personal information as well and collected meteorological information from ships at sea that was used to develop forecasts. If someone missed an area forecast, she cheerfully repeated it. In the years I fished, there was probably no one as universally loved and appreciated from the Bering Sea as Peggy Dyson.

My Beautiful Moonbow

A moonbow is a white nocturnal rainbow. It is formed by light reflected from the moon instead of direct sunlight. I was tendering salmon in Southeast Alaska with the Paragon II. My father was taking a load of salmon from Seward, Alaska to Vancouver BC with the Pelagos, and needed some parts I happened to have. We arranged to meet at the south end of Baranof Island. The seas were calm and the night quiet. I was running down Chatham Straits at around 4:00 a.m. when a glowing cotton moonbow arched over the indigo mountains of Baranof Island. I was thrilled at the unusual sight. Not recognizing it as anything I had seen before, I consulted the *Practical Navigator*, (a classic work of all things nautical by Nathaniel Bowditch), and learned about moonbows.

I awoke the crew and invited them to witness the marvelous display. They climbed to the wheelhouse where I excitedly imposed upon them the explanation of the fascinating meteorological observation overhead. They were less than impressed. Muttering curses, the disinterested men climbed back down the stairs and returned to their fleeting dreams. But I will always be grateful for my sighting of the fascinating phenomena of a moonbow. It was, for me, unforgettable.

The Green Flash

Sighting a green flash typically requires a calm, cloudless sunrise or sunset. For this reason, the Bering Sea is a poor location for viewing the rare phenomenon. I saw it at sundown while enjoying unusually placid waters in the North Pacific. The flash occurs during the final seconds of the sun's disappearance. Often, it presents only as a small green dot, ray, or shine, but that evening it lit the horizon with a sudden and spectacular green glow. And then it was gone.

That fleeting moment was my singular experience with the green flash. It was one of those unexpected events that are experienced, but not immediately comprehended. "What just happened?" I inquired of myself. "Was that the fabled green flash?" Yes, that is what I saw. "Hey everybody," I shouted to the galley. "I just saw a green flash!" No one shared my excitement.

Bow Echo

The weather was calm and cold, a delightful day for December. A pot was in the block when I noticed the black horizon—a dark expanse to the north that appeared to be quickly approaching. The radar showed a broad bow-shaped band stretching across the screen and closing fast. The crew landed the pot and went inside as I turned the boat to face the mysterious oncoming wall of weather. It engulfed us in a great grey gust of wind and rain, that rattled the rigging and scoured our ship. In a few minutes the fury faded and calm returned. The crew went back to work as the front continued its southward sweep of the sea and disappeared into the distance. The term "bow echo" refers to the bow-like shape of the radar signature accompanying a meteorological event called a mesoscale convective system like the one that just passed.

Squalls

There is an endless supply of squalls in the Bering Sea. Squalls are packages of nasty weather, or nastier weather in the midst of nasty weather. On the radar, squalls look like fuzzy balls or patches. They sometimes hide ships. Out the window, they appear as dark areas on the horizon. They can bring rain, snow, hail or just wind, but they always bring something, and it's never pleasant.

Tidal Waterfalls

Powerful tidal currents run through the passes of the Aleutian Islands. At times, the water on one side of the pass is higher than the water on the other side, and a small waterfall appears as a demarcation along the center of the pass. It is disconcerting to pass over these little falls because one normally associates the observed phenomena with rocks below the surface. The first time I saw one; I slowed the boat down and proceeded with caution, just in case the geography of the pass changed during the last earthquake.

Whirlpools

The weather was bad when I left Dutch Harbor bound for the south side of Unalaska Island via Unalga Pass. But the pass itself was a maelstrom. Strong northerly winds pushed through the narrow cut against a powerful tidal flow from the south. The result was a frothing soup of steep waves and deep whirlpools. The crew headed for their bunks.

It was my first day as captain of the Paragon II. Skirting the edge of a large whirlpool, the bow was pulled to port by the vortex. "Fantastic", I thought. "I am going to sink the boat on my first day, because I was too dumb to wait for better weather." I switched from the autopilot to hand steering for quicker control, and goosing the throttle, pulled the boat out of the eddy.

Out the forward windows, white walls of water illuminated by our flood-lights flew by in all directions. I focused on my radar and compass and tried to ignore the spouts and funnels around me. My father called on the radio. "How is it going in the pass?" he wondered.

"It's like being in a blender," I replied with obvious trepidation in my voice, "I wish you were here."

"You know what to do," he said and signed off. I made it through the pass that night, and many other rough passages since then, and I have always known what to do. A master mariner taught me well.

Current Dangers

While transiting through Seymore Narrows, a narrow channel on the Inside Passage route to Alaska, I once met a tug with two barges pushed sideways across the narrows. It was quickly bearing down on me. I was barely able to hug the beach and squeak by the last barge as the tug captain tried to swing the barges into the current and avoid disaster on an approaching reef. Seymore Narrows used to be worse. In what is described as the largest non-nuclear planned explosion before that time, Ripple Rocks, two dangerous submerged pinnacles in the narrows, were blown apart. Prior to that 1958 blast, the rocks claimed 120 vessels as victims, resulting in 114 deaths.

Buoys mark navigable channels, but they are not always reliable. The first rule of navigation is to never rely on any single source of navigation information. Since vision is a source of information, sometimes mariners should not always trust what they see. Strong currents have the ability to displace buoys that would usually indicate safe water, so familiarity with the channel and the appropriate placement of its markers is critical.

On a foggy morning as I passed through Wrangell Narrows en route to Petersburg with a load of salmon, I noticed a tug and barge approaching. Wanting to give it a wide berth, I set my course to pass close to the next buoy. The more experienced tugboat captain called on the radio and advised me to steer closer to him, as the buoy was not where it should have been.

Later that year, I was offloading salmon at the Icicle Seafoods dock in Petersburg, Alaska. The Scandies Rose, a large crab boat/tender, was anchored in the narrows. A large steel navigation buoy was dragging its anchor down the channel and heading directly for the Scandies Rose. I called the endangered vessel's captain on the radio and alerted him to the situation. If the anchor chains were to cross or the buoy hit the boat, it could cause serious problems. Almost immediately the Scandies Rose's engines fired up, and two crewmembers raced to the bow to haul the anchor. They narrowly avoided the approaching buoy and a potentially serious headache.

CHAPTER 28

JUST KIDDING

Cobra Eels and Fire Fish

Despite working around the clock and hauling hundreds of pots daily, fishing is rarely routine. That, at least, is the view from the wheelhouse. Processors standing in the same place, doing the same thing for eighteen-hours each day have a different perspective. For this reason, the ship's officers may attempt to create interest in their otherwise confined and repetitive lives.

While fishing blue king crab in Russia, the Evening Star carried four Russian scientists, a government overseer, and an interpreter. The ship's officers and the Russian scientists collaborated to create a conspiracy against the crew. The unsuspecting men were summoned to the galley for a special meeting. Speaking through the boat's interpreter, the scientists explained that a Kamchatka cobra eel, a relative of the Sakhalin fire fish, was recently sighted by a boat fishing in the area. The venomous fish often took refuge in the gill chambers of king crab, he explained. Processors should carefully avoid its painful and deadly bite.

The unsolicited testimony of a wide-eyed processor reinforced the ruse. He claimed a recent encounter with the fish described (some fish actually do enter the gill chambers of crab to deposit their eggs, but they are harmless to humans). The scientist advised that upon sighting a suspect fish, they should kill it with carbon dioxide from a fire extinguisher.

Checking the factory soon after, I noticed the processors were wearing an odd assortment of protective devices on their arms. Layers of cardboard and plastic or aluminum foil offered, they hoped, sufficient protection from the needle-sharp fangs of the fearsome fire fish. Carbon dioxide fire extinguishers were arranged within easy access of the nervous workers.

As the trip continued, concern about the Kamchatka cobra eel gradually subsided. Arm protection fell into disuse, and the fire extinguishers were returned to their proper locations. By the end of the trip, we never thought to tell the truth about the fictitious fish. For all I know, tales of the deadly denizen may still be passed among processors working in the Sea of Okhotsk.

Incredible Strength

A fully rigged crab pot weighs around 800-pounds, and it does not come with wheels. Cranes have eased much of the burden of pushing pots on the deck, but positioning a pot to land in the exact place it should go often takes too much time. Getting it in the general vicinity is good enough. From there it is pushed to its final position. There were times in my experience when the fishing was fast, and the crane was slow. Almost every pot was shoved across the deck and pushed into position.

When my cousin Jeff was a greenhorn, his first day on deck was a bit awkward. He was told to push a pot into its place against the rail and tie it down. The pot seemed glued to the wood deck boards and all of his grunting and shoving failed to persuade the stubborn pot to move. My hollering at him to hurry fueled his frustration. "Let's see you do it," he challenged. I ran over, grabbed the pot and almost effortlessly threw the heavy steel pot six feet into its place in the stack. "How did you do that?" Jeff gasped in amazement. I muttered something disparaging about greenhorns in general and went back to my work.

A few minutes later, he tried pushing the next pot, but it was equally as obstinate. When his perplexity ripened into discouragement, I taught him how to work with the roll of the boat. Moving pots is a matter of timing and leverage. Lifting the pot slightly and pushing downhill makes an eight-hundred-pound pot much more mobile. After a second demonstration, this time with teaching, he was pushing pots like a pro.

I displayed another amazing feat of strength to three temporary workers I hired to help remove some gear from the Pelagos. Among the items were five Freon cylinders that needed to be placed on the dock. I picked up the first cylinder and casually lifted it over my head. Carrying the steel tank across the deck and over the bulwark, I carefully lowered it to the dock and dusted off my hands.

"Now," I ordered, "You guys get the rest." They each grabbed one of the 400-pound cylinders, wrapped their arms around it and tried to repeat my actions. But they wouldn't budge. "What's wrong with you guys?" I chided.

"I can't even budge this thing," one of them cried. "How did you do that?"

"Well," I said, "I've been fishing crab since I was seventeen." "And," I added, after a dramatic pause, "the one I put on the dock was empty." I thought it was funny. They, not so much.

Deck Heaters and Bulkhead Screws

George was new to fishing, but not stupid. I caught him in the galley enjoying a snack when he should have been repairing a net on deck. The others, he explained, assigned him the task of locating a deck heater. He decided the deck heater sounded a lot like the fabled board stretcher, a "fool's errand." I let him stay in the galley for a while. After an hour, he returned to the deck, stating he had searched high and low for the fabled heaters, but was unable to find any.

Some greenhorns are sent in search of bulkhead screws. Any wall on a boat can be called a bulkhead, and some may be made of wood. So bulkhead screws really do exist. I never could figure that one out, but I've heard it often. Personally, I don't care for fool's errand type pranks. They lack creativity and wit.

Calibrating the Radar

Calibrating the radar is never necessary. The clever but slightly mean prank was not my creation, but I was a silent witness to its slightly sadistic implementation. With sheets of aluminum foil taped to the victim's arms, he is asked to stand on the bow with his arms outstretched while the radar is calibrated. He is told that he must not move or lower his arms until the procedure is complete. This trick will accommodate additional victims on the stern and sides of the boat as well. Eventually, the victim tires and can no longer maintain the required pose. He can be told that the calibration was successful, or that the test needs repeating, depending on how cruel one is feeling that day.

The Mail Buoy

An attempt to pull this lame gag on me occurred on the Pacific Voyager during my first year fishing crab. The victim is told to bring letters needing to be mailed to the wheelhouse as the boat would soon be stopping at the mail buoy. I was insulted. It may have been my first crab season, but I spent enough years at sea to know that mail buoys do not exist, and to know when someone was pulling a stupid joke.

CHAPTER 29

DECK DANGERS

One Hand on the Mast

The Paragon II provided some trying times, but few more terrifying to me than almost being pulled off the mast by a heavy cable. I climbed the mast to remove a shackle fastening a one-inch diameter steel cable to near the top of the mast. It was a safety cable intended to stop the fall of the picking boom if the primary lifting wire parted. I wanted to unshackle the wire from the mast and drop it slowly to the deck so the boom could be lowered for painting. But that was not how the plan played out.

I tied a line to the cable and wrapped it twice around my arm, and several times around a ladder rung, believing the arrangement would allow me to easily control the cable's descent. When I pulled the pin from the shackle, it was apparent that I had totally misjudged the weight of the wire and my ability to manage its fall. As the heavy cable dropped, the line jerked my left arm from the mast. My feet slipped from the rebar rung I was standing on, but with the grip of death, I clung to mast with my right hand. The line sizzled across my left arm cutting a sizzling spiral deep into my skin as my feet searched for a step.

Long seconds later, the cable hit the deck with a thud and I found my footing. Hugging the mast, I untangled the bloody line from my arm, amazed at my nearly fatal stupidity. Shaking, and with blood pouring from my arm, I carefully climbed down the mast. With my free hand, I bandaged my arm and cleaned the blood from the galley floor and table. My father was furious. He let me know, in so many words, that my intellect was on par with that of a flatworm. When one is stupid, being young, quick, and strong is essential to survival on a boat.

Heading home that evening, I had to ride in the back of the bouncy pick-up truck as I was still dripping blood from my aching appendage. My mom, a nurse, patched me up properly. The scar persisted for over a decade. After that incident, I bought a safety harness, and used it a few days later when I climbed the mast again to replace the cable.

Caught in a Bight

Of all the dangers of being on deck, one of the worst is working with inexperienced deckhands. When setting a pot, the floating line is tossed on top of the pot, the launcher is raised, and the pot slides overboard. A deckhand throws the sinking line after it. Then the same or another deckhand throws the buoys. Setting thousands of pots in a season, it becomes routine—until a greenhorn steps in.

One season we were shorthanded, and I was the only experienced deckhand. I was also engineer and cook, throwing the hook at every buoy, coiling every line, and setting every pot. As each pot slid over the side, the launcher was left in the up position and I threw out the sinking line and tossed the buoys. Then I lowered the launcher in preparation for the next pot. I tried to keep the others out of my way. They were only supposed to help empty the pot, stack gear, sort crab, and make bait.

My routine worked well until a greenhorn thought he would help. As I threw the sinking line after a pot, he picked up the buoys and tossed them over the side. But he tossed them behind my back, so the line was now around me. Before I could react, the line tightened and pulled me to the rail, pinning me against the launcher. With the boat running full speed, it would be mere seconds before I would be pulled overboard. A knot ran across my waist, spinning me around and battering my hips on the bulwarks. My knife was gone, torn from my belt by the sizzling line. The greenhorns stared helplessly, frozen to the deck. Frantically considering my limited options, I was about to jump overboard. I thought it better to jump and risk drowning than wait to be jerked over the side and risk severe injury as well. But the captain saw my predicament and pulled the engines out of gear. This created enough slack in the line that I was able to push it away from my waist and drop below it to the deck.

Within a few hours my hips were black and blue, and any movement was painful. During a break, I ran inside for aspirin, but it didn't help. I have never been a drug user, but as the only one with deck skills, I had to work. The pain was debilitating and I needed help. For the next week I survived on self-prescribed painkillers, working twenty-hour days while trying to manage pain without impairment. (I note that a captain has legal authority to prescribe medications at sea, including schedule C narcotics). I cannot recall a more miserable crab fishing trip.

Dealing with Danger

As a young boy riding along with Dad on the boat, I was carefree and paid little attention to the danger that surrounded me. As a twelve-year-old, a scare caused me to consider being more cautious. I was assigned to scrub the decks as the boat headed to town at the end of a trip. It was a pleasant, calm summer day and the decks were dry. I found a brand new metal bucket, attached a line and threw it over the side for some wash water. When the bucket hit the water, the line snapped from my hand, twisting my wrist, and the bucket disappeared behind the boat.

The Paragon was running only at eight knots (9.2 mph). I could easily run that fast. I thought I could effortlessly draw a bucket of water at that speed, but I was wrong. The incident should have instilled respect for safety, but I was more worried about getting in trouble for losing the shiny new galvanized bucket. I was not wearing a life jacket and could easily have been pulled overboard. I almost was. The crew was asleep. No one would have known.

As a greenhorn deckhand on a crab boat, I did what I saw others do and didn't really think about the danger. Over the years, I grew increasingly confident in my abilities, to the point of arrogance. After several seasons crab fishing, with close calls too numerous to count, I felt strong, powerful, and invincible. Every time I stepped out on deck, I felt like a fighter, with the ocean as my opponent, and I wasn't going down. I certainly wasn't scared.

Regardless of how rough it was, I felt rougher. I am fortunate to have survived my stupidity.

One day on deck, after being injured and almost pulled overboard the day before, I was leaning on the rail waiting for the captain to find the next pot. I was tired, and despite painkillers, piercing pangs shot through my body with every movement. I didn't feel invincible anymore. At twenty-six I felt old, worn out, and beaten by very hard years at sea. "If I go overboard now," I thought, "I will die."

During our next offload in Dutch Harbor, I purchased a pair of suspenders that could be inflated with a small cylinder of compressed carbon dioxide. Later I found a raincoat with a similarly inflatable pillow. Survival suits started to become common on fishing boats. I enhanced mine with a personal pack of food, water, flares, and an early type of EPIRB (Emergency Position-Indicating Radio Beacon). The more vulnerable I felt, the more I tried to increase my chances of survival.

During my years at sea, the captains of crab boats constantly put their crews in harm's way, and I was no different. Deckhands expected and recognized that working despite hazardous weather conditions, sleep deprivation, and the general dangers of the deck were necessitated by the competitive nature of the fishery. The guiding principle I used was never to ask anyone to do anything I had not done before, or be exposed to danger I hadn't faced many times myself. I am fortunate to have survived my ignorance and arrogance, but in hindsight, perhaps it was those characteristics—or character flaws—that kept me coming back to such a dangerous job.

CHAPTER 30

SEEING THINGS

Hallucinations

When I became a captain, I discovered how much more difficult it is to stay awake in a warm wheelhouse than on deck. The crew could nap between strings. I kept driving the boat. During longer seasons I generally tried to sleep a few hours every night. In good weather, we drifted and everyone slept. In rougher weather we took turns standing watch. I liked to knock off at 3:00 a.m. and start again by six or seven. When the weather was good, it was hard to stop hauling gear, but three nights without sleep was my limit. During the third sleepless night I got goofy and saw incredible things. Dancing cows and smiling pine trees were my signal to shut down for a few hours of needed rest.

The potential for problems is magnified by fatigue, but during the decades of intense competition for catch, a captain and crew not willing to work to exhaustion could not be competitive. I never hallucinated while on deck. Cold air and physical work kept me lucid right up to the point of collapse. In the wheelhouse I struggled to stay awake, and saw crazy things in a bizarre state straddling both sides of consciousness. Never at any time in my life have I used hallucinogenic drugs. Nor have I used any other illegal drugs. But I experienced, and actually enjoyed, hundreds of memorable hallucinations, working through sleepless nights with one foot firmly planted in the place of dreams. Here are a few of my favorites:

The Cottage

One sleepless night I saw a dock with a little cottage at the end. The cottage had a moss and flower covered roof. Beautiful bouquets were arranged in large pots across the front of the dock. My beautiful wife was standing at the end of the dock waving to me. Her smile was irresistible. I didn't question the presence of a flower-laden dock in the heart of the Bering Sea. It was my wife, and she beckoned me to approach. Two buoys were hanging from the dock. I brought the boat alongside, making a perfect landing. The supernal scene disintegrated when the deckhand threw the grapple at the buoys and started hauling them aboard. It was crushing to discover that the colorful cottage was a crab pot.

Singing Buoys

It was not unusual to be driving the boat down a street between buildings or through pastoral farmlands. These driving the boat on land hallucinations were the most prominent type of illusion I experienced. Sometimes I piloted the boat down a river with tall, forested mountains on each side or traveled down dirt roads with fields, farmhouses, and white picket fences. I saw city streets, and stopping at each pot was waiting at a red light. I piloted the boat over imaginary mountains, and through fields and meadows. On clear nights the silver streak of moonlight was a river, a road, or a railroad track. Some buoys had faces. Some even sang in Spanish. I was usually aware that the things I saw were fantasies, but I didn't care. To this day, I have dreams that are similar to many of the hallucinations I experienced while awake at sea.

Grandma's Friends

One night I watched the crew from the aft wheelhouse window. Who were those people and what were they doing? I could not remember. Confused, I pondered the question as I watched them work. Finally, I determined that they were picking flowers for my grandmother's friends. This made total sense, and I happily steered the boat to the next pot so they could pick some more.

Race Car Pots

Working to exhaustion was, of course, foolish. I am amazed that as irrational as my thoughts may have been, I did not make mistakes or cause accidents.

I functioned correctly, though from a fantastic viewpoint. One night the weather was rough, and I had not slept for several days. Our pots were divided between two areas thirty miles apart, and I wanted to consolidate them in the better of the areas. I determined to work until I had them all on good fishing.

As we stacked the pots on deck, the number of crab in each pot was increasing, and the deck boss called the wheelhouse to ask if I wanted to set them back. "No," I responded, "I want to move them up by our racecar pots." A picture of the area appeared on the chart table as a large oval racetrack. The pots in the better area were cars on the other side of the course, and I was trying to catch up to them. Not long after, I blacked out, re-awakening when the last pot was coming aboard. The last thing I remember was having thirty-four pots left to put on board—about three hours work. The sun was starting to rise, and beams of light shot through the wheelhouse windows as the boat pitched in turbulent seas.

I keep a list of each pot, with its unique identification number and the GPS location at which it was set. When hauling back, the pots are crossed off the list and the number of crab in the pot recorded. The last thirty-four pots were not crossed off the list, and no crab counts were recorded. But the pots were on deck. I had the crew count them just to make sure. I had no recollection of how they got there. When the crew secured the deck and came inside, the deck boss came to the wheelhouse. "That was some great driving last night," he said sincerely. "Thanks for keeping us safe." I didn't mention the fact that I had no remembrance of the previous three hours. And I was glad he didn't ask about my racecar comment.

The Milkman

On the Pacific Sun in 1993, after a large sea entered the wheelhouse and knocked out the steering, I was up for three days. On the third night, I saw large buildings on both sides of the boat. Some were set back with long canopied walkways. There were trees, people, and cars. One of the buildings was the Chicago Museum of Science and Industry, a place I visited the preceding summer.

The boat was heading down a street or parking lot area between the buildings, but instead of a boat, I was driving a milk truck and delivering milk (each stop to drop off milk was, in reality, stopping at the next buoy). After about thirty minutes of driving a milk truck, I decided I should get some sleep, so we shut down. I woke up after two hours, cold and shivering. After warming and checking with the watchman, I slept another hour. I let the crew rest a little longer. Refreshed and awake, we went back to work. It was fun being a milkman. I enjoyed the hallucination thoroughly.

Alarms

The dreams that were realities are harder to understand than the bizarre overlays of the fatigued brain. One night at sea, I was asleep in my stateroom with a deckhand on watch. I awoke suddenly from the sound of the ship's alarm. Springing from my bunk, I asked the crewman on watch what the alarm was and why he was not responding. He said he had not heard an alarm. But I clearly heard an alarm, and it woke me up.

Agitated at the disturbance, and feeling uneasy, I hurried down the three flights of stairs to the engine room. Rising water was filling the engine room bilges. I was able to start the bilge pumps and secure the flooding before the water reached anything critical (a sea-water suction valve for the bilge pump was left open and its check valve failed). Power to the alarm panel was off—apparently from an accidental and unnoticed bump of the power switch by a crewman leaving his raingear in the warm engine room to dry. There was no alarm except in my dream, and it woke me up in time to save the boat.

CHAPTER 31

SAD GOODBYES

Memorable Maydays

I have heard hundreds of mayday calls. Startling me in the day and awakening me from sleep at night, these calls are a dreaded reminder of the dangers of fishing, and the signal that somewhere, for someone, those dangers have become a horrible reality. One stormy night alone, I logged eight mayday calls and assisted with the recovery of one crew that abandoned their boat near my position.

Not all mayday calls result in the loss of life or vessel. Sometimes they are expressions of deep concern over increasingly difficult circumstances. Sometimes crews abandon their boat only to find that it did not sink after all. Other times, conditions overwhelm a captain so quickly that a mayday call is never made. Sometimes the word "Mayday" has to mean a lot more than "Help me." There is just no time to say it all. Sometimes it has to mean "Grow up strong," "Mind your mom," "Remember me," "Make me proud," "I'm sorry," "I love you," "Goodbye." Too often after "Mayday" only silence remains.

Every distress call is met with concern, and boats within range drop what they are doing and head to help. The desperate calls from friends and familiar fishing boats are the most difficult to hear. Following are my perspectives on some of the more personally poignant losses:

Vestfjord - January 29, 1989

I didn't know Dick LeGary, the captain of the Vestfjord, or any of the crew, but I knew the boat. It was designed by B.F. Jensen and built in 1969 by

Martinolich Shipyard, three years before the Paragon II. It was a sister ship to the first Bering Sea crab boat I sailed on, the Pacific Voyager.

Earlier that year they attracted attention in a Seattle shipyard. Coming out on deck after working in the engine room, I noticed that two of my crewmen were aloft in the mast. I looked around. Shipyard workers and boat crews populated masts all across the shipyard. "What the heck is everybody doing up in the rigging. What are you looking at?" I asked my men. Two lovely young ladies were sunbathing topless on the Vestfjord's wheelhouse. It brought all work in the shipyard to a full stop as men went vertical for a better view.

I will never forget the Vestfjord's mayday call. I was fishing in the Bering Sea when I heard the faint but frightening signal on the sideband. En route from Seattle to Dutch Harbor, the Vestfjord was approximately thirty miles south of the Trinity Islands (off the southern tip of Kodiak Island). They reported making ice, adding weight to the pots on deck. A few moments later, with the intensity and urgency of one facing an inevitable and tragic demise, Captain LeGary shouted, "Mayday! Mayday! Mayday! This is the Vestfjord. Mayday! Mayday! Mayday!" And then there was only static. All hands were lost.

Northwest Mariner - January 15, 1995

The Northwest Mariner was a good boat. Jim Foster was a competent captain—one of the best. The crew was as good as they came. Of all the friends and associates I lost over the years to the black depths of the Bering Sea, this was the hardest. Jim was a member of my Alaska Marketing Association Board of Directors. To make things worse, my wife was a friend of Jim's wife. It made the dangers of my occupation very real and personal for her.

With all the junk that sailed into the Bering Sea and safely sailed out again, and all the incompetent and drug-crazed captains that survived, it seems very wrong that the Northwest Mariner was lost. But something horrible went wrong on the Northwest Mariner that day. It was the opening day of snow crab season. The wind was blowing forty to fifty knots from the northeast, with seas to twenty-four feet in height. It was rough, but nothing foreign to the Northwest Mariner. I was a hundred miles to the southwest, setting my gear. There was a short mayday call and silence. Boats in the area found the overturned hull, and a life raft with two of the men inside. Neither could be resuscitated. The sinking of the Northwest Mariner was a shock to the fleet and a harsh reminder of our tenuous hold on mortality. If it could happen to Jim, it could happen to anyone.

Pacesetter – January 27, 1996

It was morning on the 25th of January, ten days past the start of the 1996 snow crab season. The crab fleet was tied up, on strike for a better price. It had been a difficult strike, and, as the fleet's negotiator, I was feeling its effects. The large processing companies rejected my price proposal, and the fleet was restless. But several small processors agreed to my offer. My task for the day was to leverage the combined processing potential of those small processors into persuading one of the larger processors to agree to my price. Once that happened, I was confident I could get the rest to comply, and the fleet could go fishing. From my room at the Grand Aleutian Hotel, I made calls, met with my Board of Directors, and dealt with the myriad of problems presented by holding back a hungry fleet of impatient crab fishermen.

At 7:00 p.m., fishermen filled the top room of the Alaska Ship Supply store in Dutch Harbor. Among them was Matt Pope, captain of the Pacesetter. Other groups of captains called in from Akutan, King Cove, and St. Paul. After some preliminary business, I was pleased to announce that the strike was over. All the processors had agreed to our asking price. For the benefit of fishermen in King Cove, the furthest port from the grounds, the Alaska Marketing Association board mandated that no pots could be set for forty-eight hours, to give all boats a chance to travel safely to the grounds.

Most of the boats left port that night. I did not. The weather was bad. I was exhausted and ill from the stress of the negotiation. With the forty-eight-hour start, there was still plenty of time to get to the grounds. As other boats, including the Pacesetter, headed out of Unalaska Bay, I took refuge in my bunk. The next morning we cast our lines and set out for the fishing grounds. The weather was now calm where I was, but still stormy to the north where the Pacesetter, overloaded with pots, rolled heavily in the steep seas.

That night it was lost, with all seven crewmembers. The Pacesetter was a 127-foot former oilrig supply vessel. When they left Dutch Harbor, they had a full load of crab pots on board, the maximum permitted by their stability report. Then they hauled twenty-seven cod pots and stacked them on top of the load. Many boats at the time used cod pots to catch fresh cod as additional bait to be used along with jars of herring. Taking the cod pots, thus exceeding their stability limits, proved a fatal mistake. By the time I reached the site of the sinking, the weather was calm. The debris field extended for a mile or two. Buoys, bait jars, and a few boards marked the watery burial spot. It was a sobering start to a crab season.

Big Valley - January 15, 2005

Gary Edwards was a good friend and one of my favorite fishermen. Friendly and gregarious, he had an easy smile and an infectious personality. He was also one of the Alaska Marketing Association's best supporters. As the Executive Director of the AMA (the collective bargaining cooperative of crab fishermen) it was often difficult for me to persuade fishermen to pay their dues. We also had an Associate Member program for businesses supporting the crab fleet. More than anyone else, Gary spent time visiting boats and businesses to collect money and memberships.

The Big Valley had stability issues. It was a smaller boat, and top-heavy. The boat got in trouble in rough seas on January 15, four hours before noon, the time they would have been able to set their pots. One crewmember was able to don an exposure suit and climb onto the Big Valley's overturned hull. When the boat finally sank, he floated for some time in the water and then spotted and eventually entered the life raft. He survived after being rescued by a Coast Guard Helicopter. Two other men were able to don exposure suits, but were not able to access the life raft, and perished. Gary and two others never even made it into exposure suits. I still have a check for $500 written by Gary the night he left Dutch Harbor. I couldn't bring myself to cash it. I kept it as a memento of a friend.

CHAPTER 32

CRAB FISHING GROWS UP

The Evolution of Sanity

In fisheries management, the term rationalization describes certain fishery management plans that result in an allocation of fisheries assets intended to curb overcapitalization, enhance economic returns, create environmental and social benefits, and improve safety of life at sea. Elements of rationalization plans may include provisions for forming harvesting cooperatives, quota shares or other restrictions to resource accessibility, and may also include provisions to protect community interests, processing sector interests, and periodic program review by the responsible regional fisheries management council.

During the 1990s, as the crab fleet continued to suffer from over-capitalization, many crab fishermen were anxious to construct a rationalization program for their fisheries. As the program for the Bering Sea crab fisheries emerged during the early years of the next decade, it included provisions for individual harvester quota shares and cooperatives, which would end the derby-style, fast as you can fishery that led to the loss of so many lives. It also provided for an individual processing quota share component intended to preserve the capital investment of crab processing companies. Measures to protect communities integral to the historical operation of the fishery were also included.

The developing program required most of the crab harvested by a holder of fishing quota to be matched with and delivered to a holder of processor quota. Competitive purchasing was limited to a small percentage of the harvest. Without the ability to move deliveries of crab to a better paying market, the program was patently anti-competitive. How would fishermen receive a fair price from a processor to whom they were obligated to deliver? To Lance Farr, President of the Alaska Crab Coalition, and myself, the answer was an arbitration system where a neutral third party resolved price and delivery term issues. The North Pacific Fisheries Management Council agreed. A committee was formed to come up with an arbitration system. John Garner, President of Norquest Seafoods, and I were appointed co-chairmen of the committee.

The committee developed two program alternatives, one developed primarily by processors (the processor by processor model), and one developed by harvesters (the fleet-wide model). The processor's plan proposed a distinct single arbitration event for each processing quota holder, potentially resulting in a different price from each processor. The harvester model would have set a single minimum price for all deliveries, regardless of the processor. The Council chose the processor by processor model. The program, described by some as the most complicated fisheries management plan in the history of fishing, went into effect in August of 2005.

That year, Gary Stewart (President of the Alaska Marketing Association) and I started the Bering Sea Arbitration Organization. Gary was President, and I became the Executive Director. All harvesters with certain types of quota shares are required to join an Arbitration Organization. Processors also organized an arbitration organization. Together, the arbitration organizations administer the arbitration system by contracting with arbitrators and a market analyst, collecting fees for program costs and implementing the system through which harvesting shares are matched with processing shares. Another harvester arbitration organization was started at the same time, but the vast majority of harvesters joined ours and the other group folded after one season.

Harvesting cooperatives formed immediately. Seventeen registered in the first year. Twelve of the cooperatives formed a common interest inter-cooperative called Inter-Cooperative Exchange (ICE). A very intelligent and capable accountant ran the group during its formative years. With the guidance of a gifted and knowledgeable attorney, several key arbitration hearings helped stabilize the program. In 2008, I was hired to manage two of the largest harvesting cooperatives. In 2009, I accepted a position as Executive Director of Inter-Cooperative Exchange. I came with a vision of uniting the twelve independent cooperatives into a single cohesive co-op. The fishermen accepted my plan and crab fishermen united as never before. Currently, ICE members harvest approximately 70% of the crab quota.

The unification of ICE led a philosophically fractured fleet toward the development of a united trade association. Alaska Bering Sea Crabbers was created as a sister organization, to address issues outside the purview of ICE. It works with fisheries management, promotes crab marketing and interfaces with the political world to enhance the safety and stability of the crab fleet and to protect the precious resource upon which our livelihood depends.

CHAPTER 33

THE DEADLIEST NO MORE

D espite the continued capitalization on the horrifying history of Bering Sea crab fishing by a sensationalistic television show, it is no longer the deadliest occupation. It is now one of the safest fisheries. Since 2005 when the crab rationalization program went into effect, until now (2016), only one crab fisherman has been lost to the Bering Sea. Several factors contribute to the Bering Sea crab fleet's new status, with the crab rationalization program being the biggest.

Another important factor was the implementation of a pre-season safety check program by the Coast Guard. New safety and survival gear, safety training and conducting emergency drills have also contributed to an emerging culture of safety that is foreign to my years of fishing.

Fishing will always be dangerous. We cannot change the weather, or prevent all accidents. But we can and have, substantially reduced the risk to fishermen. After seeing the seas most frightening faces, working past pain to numbness and utter exhaustion, and losing so many friends and fellow fishermen through the years, I am grateful for having been a part of the healing of this deadliest of fisheries.

People occasionally ask if I miss the sea. The sea is impossibly fickle and despite its beauties, it has never been a friend. Certainly I cherish my experience at sea, even and especially the dangerous and difficult times. But hanging up my captain's hat has never resulted in a moment's regret or longing. I am happy to finally be home. That chapter of my life is closed and will not reopen.

I first passed Priest Rock when I sailed into Unalaska Bay at the age of seventeen. From that time, until I brought the Valiant back to Dutch Harbor after the 1998 blue king crab season, the prominent landmark served as a symbol of passage from home, to fishing, and home again. I still frequently fly to Dutch Harbor on business, but the sight of Priest Rock no longer portends painful months away from family. I now pass the stony symbol in sacred silence, as a memorial to all who sailed past its solitary station at the tip of Unalaska Bay and never made it back. We did hard things.

Glossary

See more definitions, along with photographs, links and notes for each chapter at www.beringseacaptain.com.

American Fisheries Act: The American Fisheries Act of 1998 tightened standards of American ownership of vessels fishing in U.S. waters. It is a rationalization program that provides the Bering Sea Pollock fleet with regulations and protects non-AFA fishing sectors. It provides for the allocation of resources among the AFA sectors and allows the formation of cooperatives.

Auxiliary engine: An engine that runs a generator to provide electrical power on the boat.

Bairdi crab: Chionecetes bairdi. A species of tanner crab related to opilio snow crab but typically growing to a larger size. Bairdi is prized for its distinctive sweet flavor profile. Bairdi are found on the same fishing grounds as red king crab and opilio.

Bait chopper: A hydraulically driven device that macerates frozen blocks of herring into a mash that is filled into perforated plastic jars or pitchers. Bait choppers have removed the digits of a few careless crewmen.

Block: A hydraulically driven device that hauls in the crab pot buoy line. Two rotating metal wheels (or sheaves) are fit together to form a V-shaped groove in the center. Knots and tangles can cause the line to skip out of the block, creating a dangerous situation on deck.

Blue king crab: Paralithodes platypus. In Alaskan waters, blue king crab live around St. Matthew Island and the Pribilof Islands. In the Sea of Okhotsk, they are found in deeper waters than in Alaska. Most are dark blue or purplish on top with highlights of gold. They turn red when cooked.

Boat (or is it a ship?): Ships are big. Boats are small. The terms are interchangeable for everything in between. Some references suggest that a ship can carry a boat but a boat cannot carry a ship. Even large ships are sometimes affectionately called boats.

Boneyard: An area of seabed devoid of what one is trying to catch.

Bow thruster: Some boats have a hydraulic or engine driven propeller situated in a horizontal tunnel penetrating the hull at the bow. This propeller pushes the bow from side to side and makes docking and maneuvering much easier.

Brailer: A device for unloading crab or fish. There are numerous designs, but most involve a metal frame covered with web that can open at the bottom with the pull of a line.

Bulkhead: A boat's version of a wall.

Bulwarks: On deck, the bulwarks are a raised wall around the deck's perimeter.

Chafing gear: An arrangement of lines or fibers attached to the bottom of a net or cod end to prevent abrasion of the web on the seabed.

Charter: A contract with a government agency or private party to use a boat for a specific purpose.

Choke strap: A heavy cable near the top of a cod end that tightens around the cod end and is used to pull it up a stern ramp.

Cod end: A cod end is the detachable terminal portion of the net. It is called a cod end regardless of the presence or absence of codfish. The terms sole end, pollock end, or water end, are never used, even though they may more accurately describe the cod end's contents.

Coiler: A hydraulic device that receives buoy line from crab block and coils it in a metal barrel.

Crane: Most Bering Sea fishing boats have straight or knuckle-boom telescoping deck cranes. No certification, training, or licensing is required to operate a crane on a rolling and pitching boat.

Crows Nest: An enclosed or partially enclosed structure in the mast used as a lookout point.

Dead reckoning: Calculating one's position at sea by estimating the direction and distance traveled instead of using landmarks, astronomical observations, or electronic aids to navigation.

Deck: A boat's version of a floor.

Deckhead: A boat's version of a ceiling.

Dog: A device that keeps a winch or net reel from slacking out or paired clamps (dogs) on a pot launcher. On a crab pot launcher a dog on each side of the launcher clamps over the bottom bar of the pot to help prevent it from falling off the launcher when the pot is raised vertically for emptying.

Following sea: When a boat is travelling the same direction as the waves, it is said to be running in a following sea.

Fo'c's'le: A slight shortening of the word forecastle, a covered or enclosed area of the bow. This book uses the word forepeak in its place due to a shortage of apostrophes, and because that's what fishermen call it these days. On the old Paragon, the Fo'c's'le was a crews quarters below deck in the bow, typical of halibut schooners of its time.

Forepeak: A term used interchangeably with fo'c's'le.

Free surface effect: A slack tank has free surface effect. The weight of the water accumulates on one side and can capsize a boat.

Gale: A strong wind. The U.S. National Weather Service defines a gale as sustained winds between thirty-four and forty-seven knots. Fishermen use the term loosely.

Gear: A number of things on a boat are referred to as gear. The word can refer to fishing gear, mechanical things, apparel, pots, or nets. Or, it can refer to the reduction gear, the transmission between the engine and the shaft.

Gilson: A deck winch used to pull a cod end up a stern ramp.

Golden king crab: Lithodes aequispinus. Golden king crab are fished in the deeper waters (200+ fathoms) of the western Aleutian Islands. Golden king crab also occurs in other areas of Alaska and the Russian Far East. The legs are longer and skinnier than those of its red or blue king crab cousins. The shell is a golden brown on top but turns orange-red when cooked. It is less expensive than red king crab and stores often sell it simply as Alaskan king crab. It tastes great!

Hawser: A thick line usually used for mooring or towing another vessel.

Helm: A steering mechanism to turn the rudder. A helm can be manually operated, powered by electro-hydraulic means, or both.

Hook: A small grapple used to retrieve buoys.

ICE: Inter-Cooperative Exchange—the super-cooperative of crab harvesters. ICE vessels typically harvest approximately 70% of the annual quotas for the rationalized crab fisheries of the Bering Sea and Aleutian Islands.

IFQ: Individual Fishing Quota. Allocations of IFQ convert to pounds of crab that may be caught by the IFQ owner or leased to someone else. Members of cooperatives contribute their IFQ to the cooperative and it is allocated and managed by the cooperative. Fishermen know how much is available for each boat to catch before the season begins. There is no longer a race to catch as much as possible in as short a time as possible. IFQ was first issued in for the Bering Sea crab fisheries in 2005.

IPQ: Individual Processing Quota. Processor quota is matched with harvester quota. Crab caught under matched IFQ must be delivered to the IPQ holder it is matched with. Around 87% of the crab quota must be matched with and delivered to holders of IPQ.

Jewelry: Cables and shackles used for transferring a cod end.

Jog stick: An electric steering lever.

Jogging: Heading slowly into heavy seas – usually with just enough speed to maintain steerage.

Joint venture: In Bering Sea fishing, a joint venture was a cooperative agreement where Americans harvested fish in federally managed waters of the Bering Sea. The fish was delivered to foreign processing ships. Joint venture operations also extended to the West Coast hake fishery.

Launcher: A hydraulically driven device that lifts a crab pot over a boat's bulwark, allowing it to slide overboard. Double action launchers also lift the pot vertically so crab fall out onto a sorting table. Violent hydraulic shaking of the launcher helps dislodge crab from the pot, but also carries a risk of the pot coming off the launcher and onto the deck or sorting table, where it can crush crab or human beings. Hydraulic clamps, called dogs help prevent the pot from falling off the launcher. Despite the dogs, pots sometimes fall off the launcher anyway.

Line (or is it a rope?): Rope is for cowboys. Fishermen use line. I don't know about fishermen elsewhere but line is the term used predominantly in the

Bering Sea. An exception to this is found in the nomenclature of certain parts of a net, like headrope or footrope.

Loran: A navigation system using the triangulation of radio waves. It was developed during World War II and was used until being supplanted by GPS. My first experience with Loran was learning to chart my position with the Loran A on the old Paragon. Dials were turned until a sine wave on an oscilloscope was centered. Later models of Loran C calculated latitude and longitude automatically, but still not precisely.

Magnuson-Stevens Act: The Magnuson-Stevens Fisheries Conservation and Management Act of 1976 is the primary body of law governing fisheries management in the federal waters of the United States.

Main engine: The primary propulsion engine. Boats either have one main engine or two. Typically (but not always) boats with a forward house have one main engine (single screw) and boats with an aft house have two (twin screw).

Net reel: A hydraulic reel on the deck of a trawler that sets, hauls, and stores a net. Most Bering Sea trawlers have two or three net reels.

Opilio crab: Chionecetes opilio. A species of tanner crab that do not grow as large as the related bairdi crab. Relative abundance makes this delicious crab accessible and affordable.

Pelican hook: A hook that can be released while carrying a load. A cod end transfer wire is held in a pelican hook until it is released with the swing of a sledge hammer.

Red king crab: Paralithodes camtschaticus. The king of king crab. Most red king crab from Alaska is harvested from the pristine waters of Bristol Bay. It occurs in many areas of Alaska, the Russian Far East, the Barents Sea, and

Norway. Other types of king crab fished commercially in the Bering Sea include golden king crab and blue king crab. The tops of the shells are more purple than red, but turn red when cooked.

Running: A synonym for travelling. Fishing boats run from one place to another.

Schooner: To Bering Sea fishermen a schooner is any boat with the house on the stern. The word may have other meanings in the world of sailboats.

Sea lion buoy: Early crab fishermen around Kodiak found that sea lions sometimes bit their buoys, deflating them. Lost pots were frequently blamed on sea lion bites. A Polyfoam sea lion buoy was used to save the pot if the air-filled buoys were punctured. They were later used to prevent losing pots due to flattening when the buoys were pulled underwater by strong tides in the passes of the Aleutian Islands, or when the buoy setup was cut off by a passing boat. They are no longer used to the extent they once were.

Ship: See boat.

Shot: A length of line or anchor chain. Shots of line used by crab boats are either twenty-five or thirty-three fathoms in length. A typical crab pot is fit with one shot of three-quarters or five-eighths floating (polypropylene) line attached to the pot and one shot of three-quarters or five-eighths sinking (nylon) line attached to buoys.

Single: A simple boom and winch assembly with a single hoist wire or line.

Single screw: Having one propeller.

Snow crab: A group of crab including opilio, bairdi, and their relatives (often called tanner crab). Bering Sea crab fishermen refer to opilio as snow crab and bairdi as bairdi or tanners.

Soak: The time a pot is left on the bottom is its soak time. Sufficient soak is required for pots to fish properly. After working two or three days without sleep, letting the gear soak was often an excuse to take a nap. Being exhausted was apparently not a good enough reason. With crab rationalization, soak times have increased, allowing more time for smaller crab to exit the pot and avoid being needlessly handled.

Squall: A patch or period of weather conditions that can be a little or a lot worse than prevailing conditions. Squalls can be seen on the radar, and visually. They may carry rain, snow, wind, or hail, but we never experience a squall of sunshine.

Stack: The load of pots on the deck of a crab boat. To stack on top is to lay horizontal layers of pots on top of vertical pots in the first layer. Pots are tied with short pieces of line called pot ties. If the vessel is running for some distance, chains are used to help stabilize the stack.

Storm: According to the National Weather Service a storm is indicated by winds from forty-eight to sixty-three knots. Fishermen may refer to any bad weather, from a gale to a hurricane, as a storm. When my oldest daughter was seven or eight, I took her on a trip sailing the Pelagos from Seattle to Portland. Off the coast of Washington, we encountered hurricane force winds. It was too rough to enter the Columbia River and we waited for two days for the forty-foot seas to subside. She had fun at first—it was like being on a roller coaster ride. But when the roller coaster didn't stop, seasickness set in. She would never go with me again. Even in the flat calm waters of the river it took some convincing to get her out of her bunk. For Bering Sea fishermen, storms and hurricanes are routine.

String: A line of crab pots. A typical string might include thirty to sixty pots set five to ten pots per mile, according to the perceived density of crab in the area.

Swim bladder: A gas-filled organ found in bony fishes that helps them float or swim at a desired depth in the water column without expending energy to maintain the depth.

Tank check: Part of a pre-season ritual required by regulation. An Alaska Department of Fish and Game person checks documents and looks into tanks. They check for any crab that may have been caught by illegal pre-season fishing.

Tanner crab: A group of crab including opilio, bairdi, and their relatives (often called snow crab).

Tender (tendering): Salmon and herring harvesters typically do not deliver their fish directly to a processing facility. Instead they unload to a tender vessel. The tender may take deliveries from several harvesting boats and transport the fish to the processor. Many tenders are dedicated to that purpose. Others are crab boats, or other vessels that tender during the summer months.

Third wire: A coaxial cable used by trawlers to carry information from a transducer on the head rope of a net to the wheelhouse. The wire is spooled on a special winch. I recall spending many hours repairing and splicing broken or damaged third-wire cable. More recently a stronger armored cable has reduced repair time considerably.

Trawl: A net towed behind a boat. There are many types of trawls, designed for particular species or terrains.

Trawl door: Steel structures towed at the end of trawl cables to which the net attaches. Doors are designed to spread the opening of the net.

Twin screw: Having two propellers.

Watch: A turn driving the boat. A common watch period is two hours. On the Paragon II while trawling off the coast of Washington, we had been almost two days without sleep and were heading in to Seattle. I had the first watch. After my two hours I called my replacement. Ten minutes later I called him again. Ten minutes later I called him a third time. I finally gave up and took his watch. Calling the next two guys had the same result. Finally, the captain came stumbling out of his stateroom. "Are you on watch again," he asked.

"I never got off watch," I replied. "I couldn't get anyone up." On a boat there are few offenses as serious as failing to get up when called. The captain was furious. He stormed down to the staterooms and screamed everyone on the boat instantly awake. He was also mad at me for standing watch so long.

Web: The mesh fabric from which nets and cod ends are constructed. In repairing a net, a piece of web may be sewn into net to replaced damaged web.

Winch: A lifting or pulling device. Fishing vessels in the Bering Sea primarily use hydraulic winches.

AUTHOR BIOGRAPHY

Captain Jake Jacobsen started sailing at seven, accompanying his father on his fishing boat. At fifteen, he worked on the largest factory trawler in the United States. At seventeen, he found a job fishing crab in the Bering Sea. The next year, he was an engineer, and a few years later, a captain.

During five decades in the fishing industry, he has captained boats in all of the major Bering Sea fisheries and some of the West Coast fisheries. His experience includes trawling, crab fishing, long-lining, fish tendering, running a tugboat, participating in research charters, and working as a price negotiator.

He currently works as a marine surveyor and as executive director of the largest cooperative of Bering Sea crab fishermen. Additionally, he is a member of the Alaska Seafood Marketing Institute's Shellfish Committee, and he continues to serve, after almost a decade, on a federal advisory committee for fishing vessel safety.

97461045R00127

Made in the USA
Columbia, SC
17 June 2018